MEDITERRANEAN DIET

Cookbook

for Beginner 2023

The Upgrade Guide of Mediterranean with 6 Weeks Meal Plan | Delicious, Flavorful Recipes for Lifelong Health and Effortless Weight Loss

Melody A. Smith

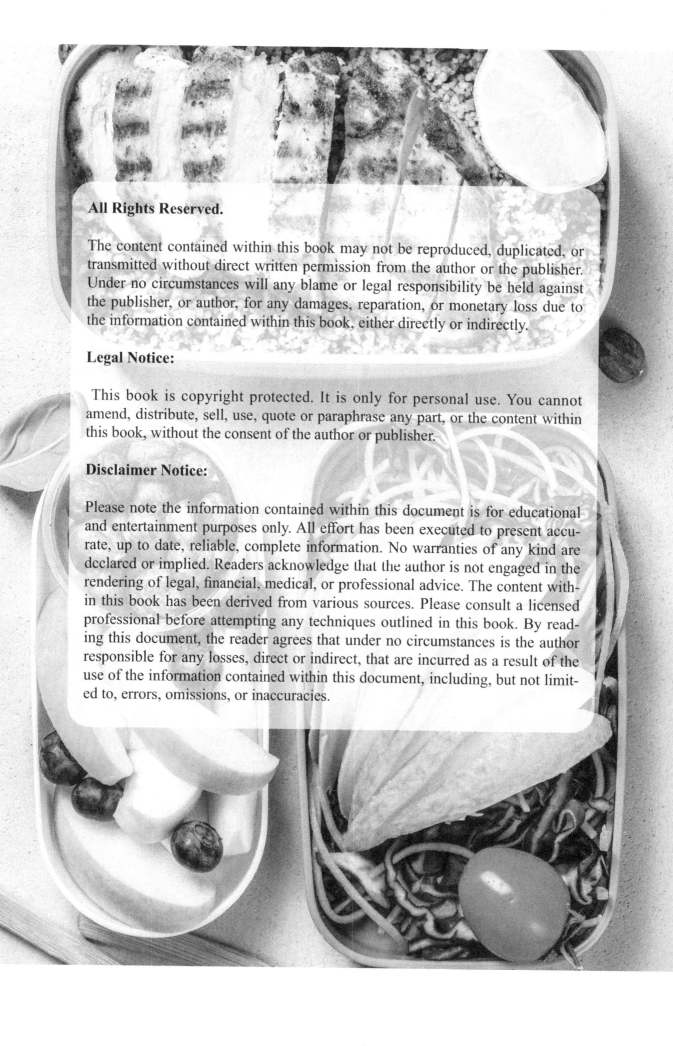

CONTENTS

INTRODUCTION

The allure of the Mediterranean has always been more than its sun-kissed shores and vibrant landscapes; it' deeply intertwined with its rich culinary tapestry that nourishes both the body and soul. Richard C. Kay, in hi exquisite offering, "The Mediterranean Diet Cookbook," presents not just a collection of recipes but an invitatior to embrace a lifestyle that has enchanted health enthusiasts and gourmands alike.

It's no secret that the Mediterranean diet has garnered accolades from nutritionists around the globe for its healtl benefits. Yet, in Richard's hands, it transforms from a mere diet into an experience. Each page of this cookbool unveils a story, an exploration into the villages and towns where these dishes originated, and a testament to the age-old belief that what's good for the soul can indeed be good for the heart.

As you navigate through this culinary compendium, Richard C. Kay promises more than just a meal. He offers a voyage—a voyage that sails through the turquoise waters of the Mediterranean, making stops at its bustling mar-kets, tranquil olive groves, and festive dinner tables.

Let's embark on this delicious journey together, savoring the secrets and stories of the Mediterranean, curatec and presented by a true aficionado.

What are the benefits of this Mediterranean diet cookbook?

Heart-Healthy Recipes

The Mediterranean diet is renowned for its cardiovascular benefits, and the cookbook offers a plethora of heart-healthy recipes to help reduce the risk of heart diseases.

Rich in Nutrients

With a focus on fresh fruits, vegetables, whole grains, and lean proteins, the cookbook provides recipes that are nutrient-dense and packed with essential vitamins and minerals.

Weight Management

Many of the recipes promote satiety and are naturally lower in unhealthy fats and sugars, aiding in weight management and overall health.

Cognitive Health

The Mediterranean diet has been linked to improved brain function and reduced risk of cognitive decline. The cookbook guides you to meals that support a healthy mind.

Diverse Flavor Profiles

From zesty lemon-infused dishes to rich olive oil drizzles, the cookbook introduces you to a wide range of flavors and cuisines, ensuring you never get bored.

Easy-to-Follow

Designed for both beginners and experienced cooks, the cookbook offers step-by-step instructions, making it easier to adopt this healthful diet.

Supports Longevity

Embracing the recipes from the Mediterranean Diet Cookbook can contribute to increased life expectancy and improved quality of life.

Reduction in Chronic Diseases

Regular consumption of Mediterranean diet recipes can lead to reduced risks of certain cancers, diabetes, and other chronic conditions.

Holistic Well-being

Beyond just physical health, the Mediterranean diet also emphasizes the importance of enjoying meals with family and friends, promoting mental and emotional well-being.

• Vegetables

Such as tomatoes, broccoli, kale, spinach, onions, cauliflower, carrots, Brussels sprouts, cucumbers, and more.

• Fruits

Including oranges, apples, bananas, strawberries, grapes, dates, figs, melons, and peaches.

• Whole Grains

Foods like whole oats, brown rice, rye, barley, corn, bulgur, whole wheat, whole grain bread, and pasta.

• Legumes

Lentils, pulses, beans, peas, chickpeas, and other types.

• Nuts and Seeds

Almonds, walnuts, Macadamia nuts, hazelnuts, cashews, sunflower seeds, sesame seeds, and more.

• Fish and Seafood

Salmon, sardines, trout, tuna, mackerel, shrimp, oysters, clams, crab, mussels, etc. It's recommended to eat fish at least twice a week.

• Poultry

Chicken, duck, turkey, etc.

• Eggs

From chicken, quail, and ducks.

• Dairy

Mainly cheese and yogurt. Greek or plain yogurt, feta, cottage cheese, and other cheese varieties are common.

- **Herbs and Spices**

Garlic, basil, mint, rosemary, sage, nutmeg, cinnamon, pepper, etc.

- **Healthy Fats**

Primarily from olive oil, which is a main cooking and flavoring method, but also from olives, avocados, and nuts.

- **Wine**

Consumed in moderation, usually one glass a day with meals, especially red wine.

- **Water**

As the primary beverage, ensuring adequate hydration.

- **Foods to Eat in Moderation**

Red Meat: Consumed less frequently than poultry and fish, limited to a few times a month.

- **Foods Rarely Consumed**

Sweets:Sweets, sugar-sweetened beverages, and sweet desserts are not an everyday treat and are consumed infrequently.

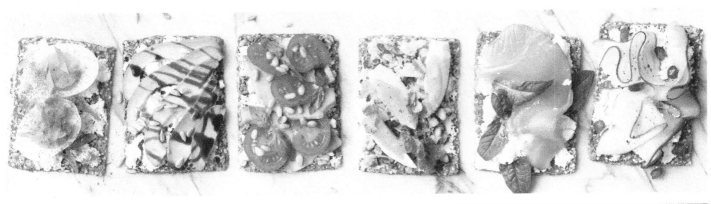

Sun-Drenched Appetizers: Begin with tapenades made from ripe olives, creamy hummus infused with tahin or stuffed vine leaves delicately spiced and drizzled with extra virgin olive oil.

Wholesome Grains and Legumes: Dive into hearty dishes like bulgur wheat salads peppered with pomegrana seeds, or slow-cooked lentil stews with a hint of aromatic herbs.

Fresh-from-the-Sea Delights: Relish in seafood treasures like grilled sardines, lemon-basted seabass, or shrim saganaki, simmered in a tomato and feta medley.

Poultry and Meat Platters: Savor the richness of dishes like herb-roasted chicken, succulent lamb kebabs, beef tagine infused with preserved lemons and olives.

Garden-Fresh Vegetables: Enjoy roasted aubergines layered in moussaka, stuffed bell peppers with rice ar herbs, or ratatouille that bursts with the flavors of the summer harvest.

Divine Dairy: Delight in the creaminess of Greek yogurt topped with honey and nuts, or sample an array cheeses from soft feta to richly textured halloumi.

Sweet Endings: Indulge in honey-soaked baklava, almond-laden semolina cake, or date-stuffed pastries that me in your mouth.

Refreshing Beverages: Quench your thirst with rose water lemonade, aromatic mint tea, or enjoy a glass of r by-red wine from the finest Mediterranean vineyards.

This Mediterranean diet cookbook offers 2,000 delicious recipes to make the most of your food. Why hesitate Hurry up and act!

6-WEEK Meal Plan

WEEK 1

Day	Breakfast	Lunch	Dinner
1	Vegetable & Hummus Bowl 13	Mushroom & Shrimp Rice 24	Feta Topped Zucchini Pancakes 47
2	Apple-oat Porridge With Cranberries 13	Easy Pork Souvlaki 35	Chicken & Mushroom Soup 47
3	Banana-blueberry Breakfast Cookies 13	Lemon Trout With Roasted Beets 25	Restaurant-style Zuppa Di Fagioli 47
4	Honey Breakfast Smoothie 14	Greek Peachy Lamb 35	Minty Lamb Egg Soup 48
5	Tuna And Olive Salad Sandwiches 14	Cheesy Smoked Salmon Crostini 25	Yogurt Cucumber Salad 48
6	Quick Pumpkin Oatmeal 14	Marsala Chicken Cacciatore Stir-fry 35	Rice Stuffed Bell Peppers 48
7	Detox Juice 15	Steamed Mussels With Spaghetti 25	Creamy Roasted Red Pepper Soup With Feta 49

WEEK 2

Day	Breakfast	Lunch	Dinner
1	Pecorino Bulgur & Spinach Cupcakes 15	Chicken Caprese 36	Orange Pear Salad With Gorgonzola 49
2	Kale And Apple Smoothie 15	Halibut Confit With Sautéed Leeks 26	Gorgonzola, Fig & Prosciutto Salad 49
3	Samosas In Potatoes 15	Chicken Cacciatore 36	Parmesan Chicken Salad 50
4	Easy Alfalfa Sprout And Nut Rolls 16	Garlic-butter Parmesan Salmon And Asparagus 26	Pecorino Zucchini Strips 50
5	Easy Pizza Pockets 16	Cannellini Bean & Chicken Cassoulet 36	Roasted Red Pepper & Olive Spread 50
6	Quick & Easy Bread In A Mug 16	Gluten-free Almond-crusted Salmon 26	Olive Tapenade Flatbread With Cheese 51
7	Creamy Vanilla Oatmeal 17	Parmesan Chicken Breasts 37	Cucumber Salad With Goat Cheese 51

WEEK 3

Day	Breakfast	Lunch	Dinner
1	Warm Bulgur Breakfast Bowls With Fruits 17	Roasted Trout Stuffed With Veggies 27	Kalamata Olive & Lentil Salad 51
2	Almond-cherry Oatmeal Bowls 17	Rosemary Pork Loin With Green Onions 37	Zoodles With Tomato-mushroom Sauce 52
3	Cherry Tomato & Zucchini Scrambled Eggs 18	Baked Fish With Pistachio Crust 27	Roasted Pepper & Tomato Soup 52
4	Maple-vanilla Yogurt With Walnuts 18	Bean & Chicken Cassoulet 37	Homemade Herbes De Provence Spice 52
5	Feta And Spinach Frittata 18	Hot Jumbo Shrimp 28	Pepper & Cheese Stuffed Tomatoes 53
6	Avocado Smoothie 19	Beef Stuffed Peppers 38	Mushroom & Parmesan Risotto 53
7	Cayenne Tomato Oatmeal 19	Salmon And Mushroom Hash With Pesto 28	Octopus, Calamari & Watercress Salad 53

WEEK 4

Day	Breakfast	Lunch	Dinner
1	Feta And Olive Scrambled Eggs 19	Slow Cooker Beef Stew 38	Feta & Cannellini Bean Soup 54
2	Artichoke & Spinach Frittata 19	Pan-fried Tuna With Vegetables 28	Sweet Chickpea & Mushroom Stew 54
3	Feta & Olive Breakfast 20	Saucy Turkey With Ricotta Cheese 38	Lemon And Spinach Orzo 54
4	Mini Pork And Cucumber Lettuce Wraps 20	Salmon In Thyme Tomato Sauce 29	Cherry, Plum, Artichoke, And Cheese Board 55
5	Cream Peach Smoothie 20	Crispy Pesto Chicken 39	Greens, Fennel, And Pear Soup With Cashews 55
6	Banana & Chocolate Porridge 21	Wine-steamed Clams 29	Favorite Green Bean Stir-fry 55
7	Falafel Balls With Tahini Sauce 21	Lamb & Paprika Cannellini Beans 39	Traditional Panzanella Salad 56

WEEK 5

Day	Breakfast	Lunch	Dinner
1	Banana Corn Fritters 22	Grilled Lemon Pesto Salmon 39	Broccoli & Garlic Stir Fry 56
2	Berry & Cheese Omelet 22	Cranberry Turkey Bake 39	Simple Mushroom Barley Soup 56
3	Pizza A La Portuguesa 82	Classic Prawn Scampi 29	Sweet Pepper Stew 58
4	Carrot & Walnut Cake 83	Panko Grilled Chicken Patties 40	Garlicky Zucchini Cubes With Mint 58
5	Mint Raspberries Panna Cotta 83	Lemony Trout With Caramelized Shallots 30	Tasty Lentil Burgers 59
6	Sweet Spiced Pumpkin Pudding 83	Grilled Lemon Chicken 40	Stir-fried Kale With Mushrooms 59
7	Chocolate-avocado Cream 84	Walnut-crusted Salmon 30	Chargrilled Vegetable Kebabs 59

WEEK 6

Day	Breakfast	Lunch	Dinner
1	Balsamic Strawberry Caprese Skewers 84	Spinach-ricotta Chicken Rolls 41	Stuffed Portobello Mushroom With Tomatoes 60
2	Spicy Hummus 85	Salmon Tartare With Avocado 30	Sweet Potato Chickpea Buddha Bowl 60
3	Orange Mug Cakes 86	Chicken Drumsticks With Peach Glaze 41	Simple Broccoli With Yogurt Sauce 60
4	Lemony Tea And Chia Pudding 86	Cod Fettuccine 31	Zucchini And Artichokes Bowl With Farro 61
5	Hummus & Tomato Stuffed Cucumbers 86	Harissa Beef Burgers 41	Authentic Mushroom Gratin 61
6	Fresh Fruit Cups 87	Mediterranean Grilled Sea Bass 31	Roasted Caramelized Root Vegetables 61
7	Cheese Stuffed Potato Skins 88	Baked Garlicky Pork Chops 42	Tahini & Feta Butternut Squash 62

Breakfast Recipes

Vegetable & Hummus Bowl

Servings:4
Cooking Time:15 Minutes

Ingredients:

- 2 tbsp butter
- 2 tbsp olive oil
- 3 cups green cabbage, shredded
- 3 cups kale, chopped
- 1 lb asparagus, chopped
- ½ cup hummus
- 1 avocado, sliced
- 4 boiled eggs, sliced
- 1 tbsp balsamic vinegar
- 1 garlic clove, minced
- 2 tsp yellow mustard
- Salt and black pepper to taste

Directions:

1. Melt butter in a skillet over medium heat and sauté asparagus for 5 minutes. Mix the olive oil, balsamic vinegar, garlic, yellow mustard, salt, and pepper in a bowl. Spoon the hummus onto the center of a salad bowl and arrange in the asparagus, kale, cabbage, and avocado. Top with the egg slices. Drizzle with the dressing and serve.

Nutrition Info:

- Info Per Serving: Calories: 392;Fat: 31g;Protein: 14g;Carbs: 22g.

Apple-oat Porridge With Cranberries

Servings:4
Cooking Time:15 Minutes

Ingredients:

- 3 green apples, cored, peeled and cubed
- 2 cups milk
- ½ cup walnuts, chopped
- 3 tbsp maple syrup
- ½ cup steel cut oats
- ½ tsp cinnamon powder
- ½ cup cranberries, dried
- 1 tsp vanilla extract

Directions:

1. Warm the milk in a pot over medium heat and stir in apples, maple syrup, oats, cinnamon powder, cranberries, vanilla extract, and 1 cup water. Simmer for 10 minutes. Ladle the porridge into serving bowls, top with walnuts, and serve.

Nutrition Info:

- Info Per Serving: Calories: 160;Fat: 3g;Protein: 6g;-Carbs: 4g.

Banana-blueberry Breakfast Cookies

Servings:4
Cooking Time: 13 Minutes

Ingredients:

- 2 medium bananas, sliced
- 4 tablespoons almond butter
- 4 large eggs, lightly beaten
- ½ cup unsweetened applesauce
- 1 teaspoon vanilla extract
- ⅔ cup coconut flour
- ¼ teaspoon salt
- 1 cup fresh or frozen blueberries

Directions:

1. Preheat the oven to 375°F. Line a baking sheet with parchment paper.
2. Stir together the bananas and almond butter in a medium bowl until well incorporated.
3. Fold in the beaten eggs, applesauce, and vanilla and blend well.
4. Add the coconut flour and salt and mix well. Add the blueberries and stir to just incorporate.
5. Drop about 2 tablespoons of dough onto the parchment paper-lined baking sheet for each cookie. Using your clean hand, flatten each into a rounded biscuit

shape, until it is 1 inch thick.

6. Bake in the preheated oven for about 13 minutes, or until the top is golden brown and a toothpick inserted in the center comes out clean.

7. Let the cookies cool for 5 to 10 minutes before serving.

Nutrition Info:

• Info Per Serving: Calories: 264;Fat: 13.9g;Protein: 7.3g;Carbs: 27.6g.

Honey Breakfast Smoothie

Servings:1
Cooking Time:10 Minutes

Ingredients:

• 1 tbsp olive oil
• 2 tbsp almond butter
• 1 cup almond milk
• ¼ cup blueberries
• 1 tbsp ground flaxseed
• 1 tsp honey
• ½ tsp vanilla extract
• ¼ tsp ground cinnamon

Directions:

1. In a blender, mix the almond milk, blueberries, almond butter, flaxseed, olive oil, stevia vanilla, and cinnamon and pulse until smooth and creamy. Add more milk or water to achieve your desired consistency. Serve at room temperature.

Nutrition Info:

• Info Per Serving: Calories: 460;Fat: 40.2g;Protein: 9g;Carbs: 20g.

Tuna And Olive Salad Sandwiches

Servings:4
Cooking Time: 0 Minutes

Ingredients:

• 3 tablespoons freshly squeezed lemon juice
• 2 tablespoons extra-virgin olive oil
• 1 garlic clove, minced
• ½ teaspoon freshly ground black pepper
• 2 cans tuna, drained
• 1 can sliced olives, any green or black variety

• ½ cup chopped fresh fennel, including fronds
• 8 slices whole-grain crusty bread

Directions:

1. In a medium bowl, whisk together the lemon juice, oil, garlic, and pepper. Add the tuna, olives and fennel to the bowl. Using a fork, separate the tuna into chunks and stir to incorporate all the ingredients.

2. Divide the tuna salad equally among 4 slices of bread. Top each with the remaining bread slices.

3. Let the sandwiches sit for at least 5 minutes so the zesty filling can soak into the bread before serving.

Nutrition Info:

• Info Per Serving: Calories: 952;Fat: 17.0g;Protein: 165.0g;Carbs: 37.0g.

Quick Pumpkin Oatmeal

Servings:4
Cooking Time:15 Minutes

Ingredients:

• ¼ cup pumpkin seeds
• ½ cup milk
• 1 cup old-fashioned oats
• 1 cup pumpkin puree
• 2 tbsp superfine sugar
• ½ tsp ground cinnamon
• 1 ¾ cups water
• ¼ tsp sea salt

Directions:

1. Place milk, salt, and 1 ¾ cups of water in a pot over medium heat and bring to a boil. Mix in oats, then lower the heat and simmer for 5 minutes, stirring periodically.

2. Let sit covered for 5 minutes more. Combine with pumpkin puree, cinnamon, and sugar. Top with pumpkin seeds and serve.

Nutrition Info:

• Info Per Serving: Calories: 143;Fat: 5.4g;Protein: 5g;Carbs: 20.8g.

Detox Juice

Servings:1
Cooking Time:5 Minutes

Ingredients:

- ½ grapefruit
- ½ lemon
- 3 cups cavolo nero
- 1 cucumber
- ¼ cup fresh parsley leaves
- ¼ pineapple, cut into wedges
- ½ green apple
- 1 tsp grated fresh ginger

Directions:

1. In a mixer, place the cavolo nero, parsley, cucumber, pineapple, grapefruit, apple, lemon, and ginger and pulse until smooth. Serve in a tall glass.

Nutrition Info:

- Info Per Serving: Calories: 255;Fat: 0.9g;Protein: 9.5g;Carbs: 60g.

Pecorino Bulgur & Spinach Cupcakes

Servings:6
Cooking Time:45 Minutes

Ingredients:

- 2 eggs, whisked
- 1 cup bulgur
- 3 cups water
- 1 cup spinach, torn
- 2 spring onions, chopped
- ¼ cup Pecorino cheese, grated
- ½ tsp garlic powder
- Sea salt and pepper to taste
- ½ tsp dried oregano

Directions:

1. Preheat the oven to 340 F. Grease a muffin tin with cooking spray. Warm 2 cups of salted water in a saucepan over medium heat and add in bulgur. Bring to a boil and cook for 10-15 minutes. Remove to a bowl and fluff with a fork. Stir in spinach, spring onions, eggs, Pecorino cheese, garlic powder, salt, pepper, and oregano. Divide between muffin holes and bake for 25

minutes. Serve chilled.

Nutrition Info:

- Info Per Serving: Calories: 280;Fat: 12g;Protein: 5g;Carbs: 9g.

Kale And Apple Smoothie

Servings:2
Cooking Time: 0 Minutes

Ingredients:

- 2 cups shredded kale
- 1 cup unsweetened almond milk
- ¼ cup 2 percent plain Greek yogurt
- ½ Granny Smith apple, unpeeled, cored and chopped
- ½ avocado, diced
- 3 ice cubes

Directions:

1. Put all ingredients in a blender and blend until smooth and thick.
2. Pour into two glasses and serve immediately.

Nutrition Info:

- Info Per Serving: Calories: 177;Fat: 6.8g;Protein: 8.2g;Carbs: 22.0g.

Samosas In Potatoes

Servings:8
Cooking Time: 30 Minutes

Ingredients:

- 4 small potatoes
- 1 teaspoon coconut oil
- 1 small onion, finely chopped
- 1 small piece ginger, minced
- 2 garlic cloves, minced
- 2 to 3 teaspoons curry powder
- Sea salt and freshly ground black pepper, to taste
- ¼ cup frozen peas, thawed
- 2 carrots, grated
- ¼ cup chopped fresh cilantro

Directions:

1. Preheat the oven to 350ºF.
2. Poke small holes into potatoes with a fork, then wrap with aluminum foil.

3. Bake in the preheated oven for 30 minutes until tender.

4. Meanwhile, heat the coconut oil in a nonstick skillet over medium-high heat until melted.

5. Add the onion and sauté for 5 minutes or until translucent.

6. Add the ginger and garlic to the skillet and sauté for 3 minutes or until fragrant.

7. Add the curry power, salt, and ground black pepper, then stir to coat the onion. Remove them from the heat.

8. When the cooking of potatoes is complete, remove the potatoes from the foil and slice in half.

9. Hollow to potato halves with a spoon, then combine the potato fresh with sautéed onion, peas, carrots, and cilantro in a large bowl. Stir to mix well.

10. Spoon the mixture back to the tomato skins and serve immediately.

Nutrition Info:

• Info Per Serving: Calories: 131;Fat: 13.9g;Protein: 3.2g;Carbs: 8.8g.

Easy Alfalfa Sprout And Nut Rolls

Servings:16
Cooking Time: 0 Minutes

Ingredients:

• 1 cup alfalfa sprouts
• 2 tablespoons Brazil nuts
• ½ cup chopped fresh cilantro
• 2 tablespoons flaked coconut
• 1 garlic clove, minced
• 2 tablespoons ground flaxseeds
• Zest and juice of 1 lemon
• Pinch cayenne pepper
• Sea salt and freshly ground black pepper, to taste
• 1 tablespoon melted coconut oil
• 2 tablespoons water
• 2 whole-grain wraps

Directions:

1. Combine all ingredients, except for the wraps, in a food processor, then pulse to combine well until smooth.

2. Unfold the wraps on a clean work surface, then spread the mixture over the wraps. Roll the wraps up

and refrigerate for 30 minutes until set.

3. Remove the rolls from the refrigerator and slice into 16 bite-sized pieces, if desired, and serve.

Nutrition Info:

• Info Per Serving: Calories: 67;Fat: 7.1g;Protein: 2.2g;Carbs: 2.9g.

Easy Pizza Pockets

Servings:2
Cooking Time: 0 Minutes

Ingredients:

• ½ cup tomato sauce
• ½ teaspoon oregano
• ½ teaspoon garlic powder
• ½ cup chopped black olives
• 2 canned artichoke hearts, drained and chopped
• 2 ounces pepperoni, chopped
• ½ cup shredded Mozzarella cheese
• 1 whole-wheat pita, halved

Directions:

1. In a medium bowl, stir together the tomato sauce, oregano, and garlic powder.

2. Add the olives, artichoke hearts, pepperoni, and cheese. Stir to mix.

3. Spoon the mixture into the pita halves and serve.

Nutrition Info:

• Info Per Serving: Calories: 375;Fat: 23.5g;Protein: 17.1g;Carbs: 27.1g.

Quick & Easy Bread In A Mug

Servings:1
Cooking Time:10 Minutes

Ingredients:

• 1 tbsp olive oil
• 3 tbsp flour
• 1 large egg
• ½ tsp dried thyme
• ¼ tsp baking powder
• ½ tsp salt

Directions:

1. In a heat-resistant ramekin, mix the flour, olive oil,

egg, thyme, baking powder, and salt with a fork. Place in the microwave and heat for 80 seconds on high. Run a knife around the edges and flip around to remove the bread. Slice in half to use it to make sandwiches.

Nutrition Info:

• Info Per Serving: Calories: 232;Fat: 22.2g;Protein: 8g;Carbs: 1.1g.

Creamy Vanilla Oatmeal

Servings:4
Cooking Time: 40 Minutes

Ingredients:

• 4 cups water
• Pinch sea salt
• 1 cup steel-cut oats
• ¾ cup unsweetened almond milk
• 2 teaspoons pure vanilla extract

Directions:

1. Add the water and salt to a large saucepan over high heat and bring to a boil.
2. Once boiling, reduce the heat to low and add the oats. Mix well and cook for 30 minutes, stirring occasionally.
3. Fold in the almond milk and vanilla and whisk to combine. Continue cooking for about 10 minutes, or until the oats are thick and creamy.
4. Ladle the oatmeal into bowls and serve warm.

Nutrition Info:

• Info Per Serving: Calories: 117;Fat: 2.2g;Protein: 4.3g;Carbs: 20.0g.

Warm Bulgur Breakfast Bowls With Fruits

Servings:6
Cooking Time: 15 Minutes

Ingredients:

• 2 cups unsweetened almond milk
• 1½ cups uncooked bulgur
• 1 cup water
• ½ teaspoon ground cinnamon
• 2 cups frozen (or fresh, pitted) dark sweet cherries
• 8 dried (or fresh) figs, chopped
• ½ cup chopped almonds
• ¼ cup loosely packed fresh mint, chopped

Directions:

1. Combine the milk, bulgur, water, and cinnamon in a medium saucepan, stirring, and bring just to a boil.
2. Cover, reduce the heat to medium-low, and allow to simmer for 10 minutes, or until the liquid is absorbed.
3. Turn off the heat, but keep the pan on the stove, and stir in the frozen cherries (no need to thaw), figs, and almonds. Cover and let the hot bulgur thaw the cherries and partially hydrate the figs, about 1 minute.
4. Fold in the mint and stir to combine, then serve.

Nutrition Info:

• Info Per Serving: Calories: 207;Fat: 6.0g;Protein: 8.0g;Carbs: 32.0g.

Almond-cherry Oatmeal Bowls

Servings:2
Cooking Time:45 Minutes

Ingredients:

• ½ cup old-fashioned oats
• ¾ cup almond milk
• ½ tsp almond extract
• ½ tsp vanilla
• 1 egg, beaten
• 2 tbsp maple syrup
• ½ cup dried cherries, chopped
• 2 tbsp slivered raw almonds

Directions:

1. In a microwave-safe bowl, combine oats, almond milk, almond extract, vanilla, egg, and maple syrup and mix well.
2. Microwave for 5-6 minutes, stirring every 2 minutes until oats are soft. Spoon the mixture into 2 bowls. Top with cherries and almonds and serve. Enjoy!

Nutrition Info:

• Info Per Serving: Calories: 287;Fat: 9g;Protein: 11g;Carbs: 43g.

Cherry Tomato & Zucchini Scrambled Eggs

Servings:4
Cooking Time:15 Minutes

Ingredients:

- 2 tbsp olive oil
- 6 cherry tomatoes, halved
- ½ cup chopped zucchini
- ½ chopped green bell pepper
- 8 eggs, beaten
- 1 shallot, chopped
- 1 tbsp chopped fresh parsley
- 1 tbsp chopped fresh basil
- Salt and black pepper to taste

Directions:

1. Warm oil in a pan over medium heat. Place in zucchini, green bell peppers, salt, black pepper, and shallot. Cook for 4-5 minutes to sweat the shallot. Stir in tomatoes, parsley, and basil.
2. Cook for a minute and top with the beaten eggs. Lower the heat and cook for 6-7 minutes until the eggs are set but not runny. Remove to a platter to serve.

Nutrition Info:

- Info Per Serving: Calories: 205;Fat: 15g;Protein: 12g;Carbs: 4g.

Maple-vanilla Yogurt With Walnuts

Servings:4
Cooking Time:10 Minutes

Ingredients:

- 2 cups Greek yogurt
- ¾ cup maple syrup
- 1 cup walnuts, chopped
- 1 tsp vanilla extract
- 2 tsp cinnamon powder

Directions:

1. Combine yogurt, walnuts, vanilla, maple syrup, and cinnamon powder in a bowl. Let sit in the fridge for 10 minutes.

Nutrition Info:

- Info Per Serving: Calories: 400;Fat: 25g;Protein: 11g;Carbs: 40g.

Feta And Spinach Frittata

Servings:2
Cooking Time: 15 Minutes

Ingredients:

- 4 large eggs, beaten
- 2 tablespoons fresh chopped herbs, such as rosemary, thyme, oregano, basil or 1 teaspoon dried herbs
- ¼ teaspoon salt
- Freshly ground black pepper, to taste
- 4 tablespoons extra-virgin olive oil, divided
- 1 cup fresh spinach, arugula, kale, or other leafy greens
- 4 ounces quartered artichoke hearts, rinsed, drained, and thoroughly dried
- 8 cherry tomatoes, halved
- ½ cup crumbled soft goat cheese

Directions:

1. Preheat the broiler to Low.
2. In a small bowl, combine the beaten eggs, herbs, salt, and pepper and whisk well with a fork. Set aside.
3. In an ovenproof skillet, heat 2 tablespoons of olive oil over medium heat. Add the spinach, artichoke hearts, and cherry tomatoes and sauté until just wilted, 1 to 2 minutes.
4. Pour in the egg mixture and let it cook undisturbed over medium heat for 3 to 4 minutes, until the eggs begin to set on the bottom.
5. Sprinkle the goat cheese across the top of the egg mixture and transfer the skillet to the oven.
6. Broil for 4 to 5 minutes, or until the frittata is firm in the center and golden brown on top.
7. Remove from the oven and run a rubber spatula around the edge to loosen the sides. Slice the frittata in half and serve drizzled with the remaining 2 tablespoons of olive oil.

Nutrition Info:

- Info Per Serving: Calories: 529;Fat: 46.5g;Protein 21.4g;Carbs: 7.1g.

Avocado Smoothie

Servings:2
Cooking Time: 0 Minutes

Ingredients:

- 1 large avocado
- 1½ cups unsweetened coconut milk
- 2 tablespoons honey

Directions:

1. Place all ingredients in a blender and blend until smooth and creamy. Serve immediately.

Nutrition Info:

- Info Per Serving: Calories: 686;Fat: 57.6g;Protein: 6.2g;Carbs: 35.8g.

Cayenne Tomato Oatmeal

Servings:4
Cooking Time:35 Minutes

Ingredients:

- 1 tbsp olive oil
- 1 cup milk
- 3 cups water
- 1 cup steel-cut oats
- 10 cherry tomatoes, halved
- 1 tsp cayenne pepper

Directions:

1. Combine milk and 3 cups of water in a saucepan over medium heat and bring to a boil. Warm the olive oil in a skillet over medium heat and sauté oats for 2 minutes.
2. Remove into the milk saucepan. Mix in oats and cherry tomatoes and simmer for 23 minutes over medium heat. Serve in bowls sprinkled with cayenne pepper and serve.

Nutrition Info:

- Info Per Serving: Calories: 180;Fat: 20g;Protein: 2g;Carbs: 4g.

Feta And Olive Scrambled Eggs

Servings:2
Cooking Time: 5 Minutes

Ingredients:

- 4 large eggs
- 1 tablespoon unsweetened almond milk
- Sea salt and freshly ground pepper, to taste
- 1 tablespoon olive oil
- ¼ cup crumbled feta cheese
- 10 Kalamata olives, pitted and sliced
- Small bunch fresh mint, chopped, for garnish

Directions:

1. Beat the eggs in a bowl until just combined. Add the milk and a pinch of sea salt and whisk well.
2. Heat a medium nonstick skillet over medium-high heat and add the olive oil.
3. Pour in the egg mixture and stir constantly, or until they just begin to curd and firm up, about 2 minutes. Add the feta cheese and olive slices, and stir until evenly combined. Season to taste with salt and pepper.
4. Divide the mixture between 2 plates and serve garnished with the fresh chopped mint.

Nutrition Info:

- Info Per Serving: Calories: 244;Fat: 21.9g;Protein: 8.4g;Carbs: 3.5g.

Artichoke & Spinach Frittata

Servings:4
Cooking Time:55 Minutes

Ingredients:

- 4 oz canned artichokes, chopped
- 2 tsp olive oil
- ½ cup whole milk
- 8 eggs
- 1 cup spinach, chopped
- 1 garlic clove, minced
- ½ cup Parmesan, crumbled
- 1 tsp oregano, dried
- 1 Jalapeño pepper, minced
- Salt to taste

Directions:

1. Preheat oven to 360 F. Warm the olive oil in a skillet over medium heat and sauté garlic and spinach for 3 minutes.

2. Beat the eggs in a bowl. Stir in artichokes, milk, Parmesan cheese, oregano, jalapeño pepper, and salt. Add in spinach mixture and toss to combine. Transfer to a greased baking dish and bake for 20 minutes until golden and bubbling. Slice into wedges and serve.

Nutrition Info:

• Info Per Serving: Calories: 190;Fat: 14g;Protein: 10g;Carbs: 5g.

Feta & Olive Breakfast

Servings:4
Cooking Time:15 Minutes

Ingredients:

• ¼ cup extra-virgin olive oil
• 4 feta cheese squares
• 3 cups mixed olives, drained
• 3 tbsp lemon juice
• 1 tsp lemon zest
• 1 tsp dried dill
• Pita bread for serving

Directions:

1. In a small bowl, whisk together the olive oil, lemon juice, lemon zest, and dill. Place the feta cheese on a serving plate and add the mixed olives. Pour the dressing all over the feta cheese. Serve with toasted pita bread.

Nutrition Info:

• Info Per Serving: Calories: 406;Fat: 38.2g;Protein: 7.9g;Carbs: 8g.

Mini Pork And Cucumber Lettuce Wraps

Servings:12
Cooking Time: 0 Minutes

Ingredients:

• 8 ounces cooked ground pork
• 1 cucumber, diced
• 1 tomato, diced
• 1 red onion, sliced
• 1 ounce low-fat feta cheese, crumbled
• Juice of 1 lemon
• 1 tablespoon extra-virgin olive oil
• Sea salt and freshly ground pepper, to taste
• 12 small, intact iceberg lettuce leaves

Directions:

1. Combine the ground pork, cucumber, tomato, and onion in a large bowl, then scatter with feta cheese. Drizzle with lemon juice and olive oil, and sprinkle with salt and pepper. Toss to mix well.

2. Unfold the small lettuce leaves on a large plate or several small plates, then divide and top with the pork mixture.

3. Wrap and serve immediately.

Nutrition Info:

• Info Per Serving: Calories: 78;Fat: 5.6g;Protein: 5.5g;Carbs: 1.4g.

Cream Peach Smoothie

Servings:1
Cooking Time:5 Minutes

Ingredients:

• 1 large peach, sliced
• 6 oz peach Greek yogurt
• 2 tbsp almond milk
• 2 ice cubes

Directions:

1. Blend the peach, yogurt, almond milk, and ice cubes in your food processor until thick and creamy. Serve and enjoy!

Nutrition Info:

• Info Per Serving: Calories: 228;Fat: 3g;Protein: 11g;Carbs: 41.6g.

Banana & Chocolate Porridge

Servings:4
Cooking Time:20 Minutes

Ingredients:

- 2 bananas
- 4 dried apricots, chopped
- 1 cup barley, soaked
- 2 tbsp flax seeds
- 1 tbsp cocoa powder
- 1 cup coconut milk
- ¼ tsp mint leaves
- 2 oz dark chocolate bars, grated
- 2 tbsp coconut flakes

Directions:

1. Place the barley in a saucepan along with the flax-seeds and two cups of water. Bring to a boil, then lower the heat and simmer for 12 minutes, stirring often.
2. Meanwhile, in a food processor, blend bananas, cocoa powder, coconut milk, apricots, and mint leaves until smooth. Once the barley is ready, stir in chocolate. Add in banana mixture. Garnish with coconut flakes. Serve.

Nutrition Info:

- Info Per Serving: Calories: 476;Fat: 22g;Protein: 10g;Carbs: 65g.

Falafel Balls With Tahini Sauce

Servings:4
Cooking Time: 20 Minutes

Ingredients:

- Tahini Sauce:
- ½ cup tahini
- 2 tablespoons lemon juice
- ¼ cup finely chopped flat-leaf parsley
- 2 cloves garlic, minced
- ½ cup cold water, as needed
- Falafel:
- 1 cup dried chickpeas, soaked overnight, drained
- ¼ cup chopped flat-leaf parsley
- ¼ cup chopped cilantro
- 1 large onion, chopped
- 1 teaspoon cumin
- ½ teaspoon chili flakes
- 4 cloves garlic
- 1 teaspoon sea salt
- 5 tablespoons almond flour
- 1½ teaspoons baking soda, dissolved in 1 teaspoon water
- 2 cups peanut oil
- 1 medium bell pepper, chopped
- 1 medium tomato, chopped
- 4 whole-wheat pita breads

Directions:

1. Make the Tahini Sauce:
2. Combine the ingredients for the tahini sauce in a small bowl. Stir to mix well until smooth.
3. Wrap the bowl in plastic and refrigerate until ready to serve.
4. Make the Falafel:
5. Put the chickpeas, parsley, cilantro, onion, cumin, chili flakes, garlic, and salt in a food processor. Pulse to mix well but not puréed.
6. Add the flour and baking soda to the food processor, then pulse to form a smooth and tight dough.
7. Put the dough in a large bowl and wrap in plastic. Refrigerate for at least 2 hours to let it rise.
8. Divide and shape the dough into walnut-sized small balls.
9. Pour the peanut oil in a large pot and heat over high heat until the temperature of the oil reaches 375°F.
10. Drop 6 balls into the oil each time, and fry for 5 minutes or until golden brown and crispy. Turn the balls with a strainer to make them fried evenly.
11. Transfer the balls on paper towels with the strainer, then drain the oil from the balls.
12. Roast the pita breads in the oven for 5 minutes or until golden brown, if needed, then stuff the pitas with falafel balls and top with bell peppers and tomatoes. Drizzle with tahini sauce and serve immediately.

Nutrition Info:

- Info Per Serving: Calories: 574;Fat: 27.1g;Protein: 19.8g;Carbs: 69.7g.

Banana Corn Fritters

Servings:2
Cooking Time: 10 Minutes

Ingredients:

- ½ cup yellow cornmeal
- ¼ cup flour
- 2 small ripe bananas, peeled and mashed
- 2 tablespoons unsweetened almond milk
- 1 large egg, beaten
- ½ teaspoon baking powder
- ¼ to ½ teaspoon ground chipotle chili
- ¼ teaspoon ground cinnamon
- ¼ teaspoon sea salt
- 1 tablespoon olive oil

Directions:

1. Stir together all ingredients except for the olive oil in a large bowl until smooth.
2. Heat a nonstick skillet over medium-high heat. Add the olive oil and drop about 2 tablespoons of batter for each fritter. Cook for 2 to 3 minutes until the bottoms are golden brown, then flip. Continue cooking for 1 to 2 minutes more, until cooked through. Repeat with the remaining batter.
3. Serve warm.

Nutrition Info:

- Info Per Serving: Calories: 396;Fat: 10.6g;Protein: 7.3g;Carbs: 68.0g.

Berry & Cheese Omelet

Servings:4
Cooking Time:10 Minutes

Ingredients:

- 2 tbsp olive oil
- 6 eggs, whisked
- 1 tsp cinnamon powder
- 1 cup ricotta cheese
- 4 oz berries

Directions:

1. Whisk eggs, cinnamon powder, ricotta cheese, and berries in a bowl. Warm the olive oil in a skillet over medium heat and pour in the egg mixture. Cook for 2 minutes, turn the egg and cook for 2 minutes more. Serve immediately.

Nutrition Info:

- Info Per Serving: Calories: 256;Fat: 18g;Protein: 15.6g;Carbs: 7g.

Fish And Seafood Recipes

Calamari In Garlic-cilantro Sauce

Servings:4
Cooking Time:25 Minutes

Ingredients:

- 2 tbsp olive oil
- 2 lb calamari, sliced into rings
- 4 garlic cloves, minced
- 1 lime, juiced
- 2 tbsp balsamic vinegar
- 3 tbsp cilantro, chopped

Directions:

1. Warm the olive oil in a skillet over medium heat and sauté garlic, lime juice, balsamic vinegar, and cilantro for 5 minutes. Stir in calamari rings and cook for 10 minutes.

Nutrition Info:

- Info Per Serving: Calories: 290;Fat: 19g;Protein: 19g;Carbs: 10g.

Mushroom & Shrimp Rice

Servings:4
Cooking Time:40 Minutes

Ingredients:

- 2 tbsp olive oil
- 1 lb shrimp, peeled, deveined
- 1 cup white rice
- 4 garlic cloves, sliced
- ¼ tsp hot paprika
- 1 cup mushrooms, sliced
- ¼ cup green peas
- Juice of 1 lime
- Sea salt to taste
- ¼ cup chopped fresh chives

Directions:

1. Bring a pot of salted water to a boil. Cook the rice for 15-18 minutes, stirring occasionally. Drain and place in a bowl. Add in the green peas and mix to combine well. Taste and adjust the seasoning. Remove to a serving plate.

2. Heat the olive oil in a saucepan over medium heat and sauté garlic and hot paprika for 30-40 seconds until garlic is light golden brown. Remove the garlic with a slotted spoon. Add the mushrooms to the saucepan and sauté them for 5 minutes until tender. Put in the shrimp, lime juice, and salt and stir for 4 minutes. Turn the heat off. Add the chives and reserved garlic to the shrimp and pour over the rice. Serve and enjoy!

Nutrition Info:

- Info Per Serving: Calories: 342;Fat: 12g;Protein: 24g;Carbs: 33g.

Drunken Mussels With Lemon-butter Sauce

Servings:4
Cooking Time:15 Minutes

Ingredients:

- 4 lb mussels, cleaned
- 4 tbsp butter
- ½ cup chopped parsley
- 1 white onion, chopped
- 2 cups dry white wine
- ½ tsp sea salt
- 6 garlic cloves, minced
- Juice of ½ lemon

Directions:

1. Add wine, garlic, salt, onion, and ¼ cup of parsley in a pot over medium heat and let simmer. Put in mussels and simmer covered for 7-8 minutes. Divide mussels between four bowls. Stir butter and lemon juice into the pot and drizzle over the mussels. Top with parsley and serve.

Nutrition Info:

- Info Per Serving: Calories: 487;Fat: 18g;Protein:

7g;Carbs: 26g.

Lemon Trout With Roasted Beets

Servings:4
Cooking Time:45 Minutes

Ingredients:

1 lb medium beets, peeled and sliced
3 tbsp olive oil
4 trout fillets, boneless
Salt and black pepper to taste
1 tbsp rosemary, chopped
2 spring onions, chopped
2 tbsp lemon juice
½ cup vegetable stock

Directions:

. Preheat oven to 390F. Line a baking sheet with parchment paper. Arrange the beets on the sheet, season with salt and pepper, and drizzle with some olive oil. Roast for 20 minutes.

. Warm the remaining oil in a skillet over medium heat. Cook trout fillets for 8 minutes on all sides; reserve. Add spring onions to the skillet and sauté for 2 minutes. Stir in lemon juice and stock and cook for 5-6 minutes until the sauce thickens. Remove the beets to a plate and top with trout fillets. Pour the sauce all over and sprinkle with rosemary.

Nutrition Info:

Info Per Serving: Calories: 240;Fat: 6g;Protein: 8g;Carbs: 22g.

Cheesy Smoked Salmon Crostini

Servings:4
Cooking Time:10 Min + Chilling Time

Ingredients:

4 oz smoked salmon, sliced
2 oz feta cheese, crumbled
4 oz cream cheese, softened
2 tbsp horseradish sauce
2 tsp orange zest
1 red onion, chopped
2 tbsp chives, chopped
1 baguette, sliced and toasted

Directions:

1. In a bowl, mix cream cheese, horseradish sauce, onion, feta cheese, and orange zest until smooth. Spread the mixture on the baguette slices. Top with salmon and chives to serve.

Nutrition Info:

• Info Per Serving: Calories: 290;Fat: 19g;Protein: 26g;Carbs: 5g.

Steamed Mussels With Spaghetti

Servings:4
Cooking Time:30 Minutes

Ingredients:

• 2 lb mussels, cleaned and beards removed
• 1 lb cooked spaghetti
• 3 tbsp butter
• 2 garlic cloves, minced
• 1 carrot, diced
• 1 onion, chopped
• 2 celery sticks, chopped
• 1 cup white wine
• 2 tbsp parsley, chopped
• ½ tsp red pepper flakes
• 1 lemon, juiced

Directions:

1. Melt butter in a saucepan over medium heat and sauté the garlic, carrot, onion, and celery for 4-5 minutes, stirring occasionally until softened. Add the mussels, white wine, and lemon juice, cover, and bring to a boil. Reduce the heat and steam the for 4-6 minutes. Discard any unopened mussels. Stir in spaghetti to coat. Sprinkle with parsley and red pepper flakes to serve.

Nutrition Info:

• Info Per Serving: Calories: 669;Fat: 16g;Protein: 41g;Carbs: 77g.

Halibut Confit With Sautéed Leeks

Servings:4
Cooking Time:45 Minutes

Ingredients:

- 1 tsp fresh lemon zest
- ¼ cup olive oil
- 4 skinless halibut fillets
- Salt and black pepper to taste
- 1 lb leeks, sliced
- 1 tsp Dijon mustard
- ¾ cup dry white wine
- 1 tbsp fresh cilantro, chopped
- 4 lemon wedges

Directions:

1. Warm the olive oil in a skillet over medium heat. Season the halibut with salt and pepper. Sear in the skillet for 6-7 minutes until cooked all the way through. Carefully transfer the halibut to a large plate. Add leeks, mustard, salt, and pepper to the skillet and sauté for 10-12 minutes, stirring frequently, until softened. Pour in the wine and lemon zest and bring to a simmer. Top with halibut. Reduce the heat to low, cover, and simmer for 6-10 minutes. Carefully transfer halibut to a serving platter, tent loosely with aluminum foil, and let rest while finishing leeks. Increase the heat and cook the leeks for 2-4 minutes until the sauce is slightly thickened. Adjust the seasoning with salt and pepper. Pour the leek mixture around the halibut, sprinkle with cilantro, and serve with lemon wedges.

Nutrition Info:

- Info Per Serving: Calories: 566;Fat: 19g;Protein: 78g;Carbs: 17g.

Garlic-butter Parmesan Salmon And Asparagus

Servings:2
Cooking Time: 15 Minutes

Ingredients:

- 2 salmon fillets, skin on and patted dry
- Pink Himalayan salt
- Freshly ground black pepper, to taste
- 1 pound fresh asparagus, ends snapped off
- 3 tablespoons almond butter
- 2 garlic cloves, minced
- ¼ cup grated Parmesan cheese

Directions:

1. Preheat the oven to 400ºF. Line a baking sheet with aluminum foil.
2. Season both sides of the salmon fillets with salt and pepper.
3. Put the salmon in the middle of the baking sheet and arrange the asparagus around the salmon.
4. Heat the almond butter in a small saucepan over medium heat.
5. Add the minced garlic and cook for about 3 minutes, or until the garlic just begins to brown.
6. Drizzle the garlic-butter sauce over the salmon and asparagus and scatter the Parmesan cheese on top.
7. Bake in the preheated oven for about 12 minutes, or until the salmon is cooked through and the asparagus is crisp-tender. You can switch the oven to broil at the end of cooking time for about 3 minutes to get a nice char on the asparagus.
8. Let cool for 5 minutes before serving.

Nutrition Info:

- Info Per Serving: Calories: 435;Fat: 26.1g;Protein: 42.3g;Carbs: 10.0g.

Gluten-free Almond-crusted Salmon

Servings:4
Cooking Time:20 Minutes

Ingredients:

- 1 tbsp olive oil
- ½ tsp lemon zest
- ¼ cup breadcrumbs
- ½ cup toasted almonds, ground
- ½ tsp dried thyme
- Salt and black pepper to taste
- 4 salmon steaks
- 1 lemon, cut into wedges

Directions:

1. Preheat oven to 350 F. In a shallow dish, combine the lemon zest, breadcrumbs, almonds, thyme, salt and pepper. Coat the salmon steaks with olive oil and arrange them on a baking sheet. Cover them with the

almond mixture, pressing down lightly with your fingers to create a tightly packed crust. Bake for 10-12 minutes or until the almond crust is lightly browned and the fish is cooked through. Serve garnished with lemon wedges.

Nutrition Info:

• Info Per Serving: Calories: 568;Fat: 28g;Protein: 66g;Carbs: 9.6g.

Roasted Trout Stuffed With Veggies

Servings:2
Cooking Time: 25 Minutes

Ingredients:

• 2 whole trout fillets, dressed (cleaned but with bones and skin intact)
• 1 tablespoon extra-virgin olive oil
• ¼ teaspoon salt
• ⅛ teaspoon freshly ground black pepper
• 1 small onion, thinly sliced
• ½ red bell pepper, seeded and thinly sliced
• 1 poblano pepper, seeded and thinly sliced
• 2 or 3 shiitake mushrooms, sliced
• 1 lemon, sliced
• Nonstick cooking spray

Directions:

1. Preheat the oven to 425°F. Spray a baking sheet with nonstick cooking spray.
2. Rub both trout fillets, inside and out, with the olive oil. Season with salt and pepper.
3. Mix together the onion, bell pepper, poblano pepper, and mushrooms in a large bowl. Stuff half of this mixture into the cavity of each fillet. Top the mixture with 2 or 3 lemon slices inside each fillet.
4. Place the fish on the prepared baking sheet side by side. Roast in the preheated oven for 25 minutes, or until the fish is cooked through and the vegetables are tender.
5. Remove from the oven and serve on a plate.

Nutrition Info:

• Info Per Serving: Calories: 453;Fat: 22.1g;Protein: 49.0g;Carbs: 13.8g.

Baked Fish With Pistachio Crust

Servings:4
Cooking Time: 15 To 20 Minutes

Ingredients:

• ½ cup extra-virgin olive oil, divided
• 1 pound flaky white fish (such as cod, haddock, or halibut), skin removed
• ½ cup shelled finely chopped pistachios
• ½ cup ground flaxseed
• Zest and juice of 1 lemon, divided
• 1 teaspoon ground cumin
• 1 teaspoon ground allspice
• ½ teaspoon salt
• ¼ teaspoon freshly ground black pepper

Directions:

1. Preheat the oven to 400°F.
2. Line a baking sheet with parchment paper or aluminum foil and drizzle 2 tablespoons of olive oil over the sheet, spreading to evenly coat the bottom.
3. Cut the fish into 4 equal pieces and place on the prepared baking sheet.
4. In a small bowl, combine the pistachios, flaxseed, lemon zest, cumin, allspice, salt, and pepper. Drizzle in ¼ cup of olive oil and stir well.
5. Divide the nut mixture evenly on top of the fish pieces. Drizzle the lemon juice and remaining 2 tablespoons of olive oil over the fish and bake until cooked through, 15 to 20 minutes, depending on the thickness of the fish.
6. Cool for 5 minutes before serving.

Nutrition Info:

• Info Per Serving: Calories: 509;Fat: 41.0g;Protein: 26.0g;Carbs: 9.0g.

Hot Jumbo Shrimp

Servings:4
Cooking Time:20 Minutes

Ingredients:

- 2 lb shell-on jumbo shrimp, deveined
- ¼ cup olive oil
- Salt and black pepper to taste
- 6 garlic cloves, minced
- 1 tsp anise seeds
- ½ tsp red pepper flakes
- 2 tbsp minced fresh cilantro
- 1 lemon, cut into wedges

Directions:

1. Combine the olive oil, garlic, anise seeds, pepper flakes, and black pepper in a large bowl. Add the shrimp and cilantro and toss well, making sure the oil mixture gets into the interior of the shrimp. Arrange shrimp in a single layer on a baking tray. Set under the preheated broiler for approximately 4 minutes. Flip shrimp and continue to broil until it is opaque and shells are beginning to brown, about 2 minutes, rotating sheet halfway through broiling. Serve with lemon wedges.

Nutrition Info:

- Info Per Serving: Calories: 218;Fat: 9g;Protein: 30.8g;Carbs: 2.3g.

Salmon And Mushroom Hash With Pesto

Servings:6
Cooking Time: 20 Minutes

Ingredients:

- Pesto:
- ¼ cup extra-virgin olive oil
- 1 bunch fresh basil
- Juice and zest of 1 lemon
- ⅓ cup water
- ¼ teaspoon salt, plus additional as needed
- Hash:
- 2 tablespoons extra-virgin olive oil
- 6 cups mixed mushrooms (brown, white, shiitake, cremini, portobello, etc.), sliced
- 1 pound wild salmon, cubed

Directions:

1. Make the pesto: Pulse the olive oil, basil, juice and zest, water, and salt in a blender or food processor until smoothly blended. Set aside.
2. Heat the olive oil in a large skillet over medium heat.
3. Stir-fry the mushrooms for 6 to 8 minutes, or until they begin to exude their juices.
4. Add the salmon and cook each side for 5 to 6 minutes until cooked through.
5. Fold in the prepared pesto and stir well. Taste and add additional salt as needed. Serve warm.

Nutrition Info:

- Info Per Serving: Calories: 264;Fat: 14.7g;Protein: 7.0g;Carbs: 30.9g.

Pan-fried Tuna With Vegetables

Servings:4
Cooking Time:25 Minutes

Ingredients:

- 2 tbsp olive oil
- 4 tuna fillets, boneless
- 1 red bell pepper, chopped
- 1 onion, chopped
- 4 garlic cloves, minced
- ½ cup fish stock
- 1 tsp basil, dried
- ½ cup cherry tomatoes, halved
- ½ cup black olives, halved
- Salt and black pepper to taste

Directions:

1. Warm the olive oil in a skillet over medium heat and fry tuna for 10 minutes on both sides. Divide the fish among plates. In the same skillet, cook onion, bell pepper, garlic, and cherry tomatoes for 3 minutes. Stir in salt, pepper, fish stock, basil, and olives and cook for another 3 minutes. Top the tuna with the mixture and serve immediately.

Nutrition Info:

- Info Per Serving: Calories: 260;Fat: 9g;Protein: 29g;Carbs: 6g.

Salmon In Thyme Tomato Sauce

Servings:4
Cooking Time:25 Minutes

Ingredients:

- 2 tbsp olive oil
- 4 salmon fillets, boneless
- 1 tsp thyme, chopped
- Salt and black pepper to taste
- 1 lb cherry tomatoes, halved

Directions:

1. Warm the olive oil in a skillet over medium heat and sear salmon for 6 minutes, turning once; set aside. In the same skillet, stir in cherry tomatoes for 3-4 minutes and sprinkle with thyme, salt, and pepper. Pour the sauce over the salmon.

Nutrition Info:

- Info Per Serving: Calories: 300;Fat: 18g;Protein: 26g;Carbs: 27g.

Wine-steamed Clams

Servings:4
Cooking Time:30 Minutes

Ingredients:

- 4 lb clams, scrubbed and debearded
- 3 tbsp butter
- 3 garlic cloves, minced
- ¼ tsp red pepper flakes
- 1 cup dry white wine
- 3 sprigs fresh thyme
- 2 tbsp fresh dill, minced

Directions:

1. Melt the butter in a large saucepan over medium heat and cook garlic and pepper flakes, stirring constantly, until fragrant, about 30 seconds. Stir in wine and thyme sprigs, bring to a boil and cook until wine is slightly reduced, about 1 minute. Stir in clams. Cover the saucepan and simmer for 15-18 minutes. Remove, discard thyme sprigs and any clams that refuse to open. Sprinkle with dill and serve.

Nutrition Info:

- Info Per Serving: Calories: 326;Fat: 14g;Protein: 36g;Carbs: 12g.

Grilled Lemon Pesto Salmon

Servings:2
Cooking Time: 6 To 10 Minutes

Ingredients:

- 10 ounces salmon fillet
- Salt and freshly ground black pepper, to taste
- 2 tablespoons prepared pesto sauce
- 1 large fresh lemon, sliced
- Cooking spray

Directions:

1. Preheat the grill to medium-high heat. Spray the grill grates with cooking spray.
2. Season the salmon with salt and black pepper. Spread the pesto sauce on top.
3. Make a bed of fresh lemon slices about the same size as the salmon fillet on the hot grill, and place the salmon on top of the lemon slices. Put any additional lemon slices on top of the salmon.
4. Grill the salmon for 6 to 10 minutes, or until the fish is opaque and flakes apart easily.
5. Serve hot.

Nutrition Info:

- Info Per Serving: Calories: 316;Fat: 21.1g;Protein: 29.0g;Carbs: 1.0g.

Classic Prawn Scampi

Servings:4
Cooking Time:25 Minutes

Ingredients:

- 1 lb prawns, peeled and deveined
- 2 tbsp olive oil
- 1 onion, chopped
- 6 garlic cloves, minced
- 1 lemon, juiced and zested
- ½ cup dry white wine
- Salt and black pepper to taste
- 2 cups fusilli, cooked
- ½ tsp red pepper flakes

Directions:

1. Warm olive oil in a pan over medium heat and sau-

té onion and garlic for 3 minutes, stirring often, until fragrant. Stir in prawns and cook for 3-4 minutes. Mix in lemon juice, lemon zest, salt, pepper, wine, and red flakes. Bring to a boil, then decrease the heat, and simmer for 2 minutes until the liquid is reduced by half. Turn the heat off. Stir in pasta and serve.

Nutrition Info:

• Info Per Serving: Calories: 388;Fat: 9g;Protein: 32g;Carbs: 38.2g.

Lemony Trout With Caramelized Shallots

Servings:2
Cooking Time: 20 Minutes

Ingredients:

• Shallots:
• 1 teaspoon almond butter
• 2 shallots, thinly sliced
• Dash salt
• Trout:
• 1 tablespoon plus 1 teaspoon almond butter, divided
• 2 trout fillets
• 3 tablespoons capers
• ¼ cup freshly squeezed lemon juice
• ¼ teaspoon salt
• Dash freshly ground black pepper
• 1 lemon, thinly sliced

Directions:

1. Make the Shallots
2. In a large skillet over medium heat, cook the butter, shallots, and salt for 20 minutes, stirring every 5 minutes, or until the shallots are wilted and caramelized.
3. Make the Trout
4. Meanwhile, in another large skillet over medium heat, heat 1 teaspoon of almond butter.
5. Add the trout fillets and cook each side for 3 minutes, or until flaky. Transfer to a plate and set aside.
6. In the skillet used for the trout, stir in the capers, lemon juice, salt, and pepper, then bring to a simmer. Whisk in the remaining 1 tablespoon of almond butter. Spoon the sauce over the fish.
7. Garnish the fish with the lemon slices and caramelized shallots before serving.

Nutrition Info:

• Info Per Serving: Calories: 344;Fat: 18.4g;Protein: 21.1g;Carbs: 14.7g.

Walnut-crusted Salmon

Servings:4
Cooking Time:25 Minutes

Ingredients:

• 2 tbsp olive oil
• 4 salmon fillets, boneless
• 2 tbsp mustard
• 5 tsp honey
• 1 cup walnuts, chopped
• 1 tbsp lemon juice
• 2 tsp parsley, chopped
• Salt and pepper to the taste

Directions:

1. Preheat the oven to 380F. Line a baking tray with parchment paper. In a bowl, whisk the olive oil, mustard, and honey. In a separate bowl, combine walnuts and parsley. Sprinkle salmon with salt and pepper and place them on the tray. Rub each fillet with mustard mixture and scatter with walnut mixture; bake for 15 minutes. Drizzle with lemon juice.

Nutrition Info:

• Info Per Serving: Calories: 300;Fat: 16g;Protein: 17g;Carbs: 22g.

Salmon Tartare With Avocado

Servings:4
Cooking Time:10 Minutes + Chilling Time

Ingredients:

• 1 lb salmon, skinless, boneless and cubed
• 1 tbsp olive oil
• 4 tbsp scallions, chopped
• 2 tsp lemon juice
• 1 avocado, chopped
• Salt and black pepper to taste
• 1 tbsp parsley, chopped

Directions:

1. Mix scallions, lemon juice, olive oil, salmon, salt

pepper, and parsley in a bowl. Place in the fridge for 1 hour. Place a baking ring on a serving plate and pour in the salmon mixture. Top with avocado and gently press down. Serve.

Nutrition Info:

• Info Per Serving: Calories: 230;Fat: 15g;Protein: 6g;Carbs: 13g.

Cod Fettuccine

Servings:4
Cooking Time:30 Minutes

Ingredients:

• 1 lb cod fillets, cubed
• 16 oz fettuccine
• 3 tbsp olive oil
• 1 onion, finely chopped
• Salt and lemon pepper to taste
• 1 ½ cups heavy cream
• 1 cup Parmesan cheese, grated

Directions:

1. Boil salted water in a pot over medium heat and stir in fettuccine. Cook according to package directions and drain. Heat the olive oil in a large saucepan over medium heat and add the onion. Stir-fry for 3 minutes until tender. Sprinkle cod with salt and lemon pepper and add to saucepan; cook for 4–5 minutes until fish fillets and flakes easily with a fork. Stir in heavy cream for 2 minutes. Add in the pasta, tossing gently to combine. Cook for 3–4 minutes until sauce is slightly thickened. Sprinkle with Parmesan cheese.

Nutrition Info:

• Info Per Serving: Calories: 431;Fat: 36g;Protein: 42g;Carbs: 97g.

Mediterranean Grilled Sea Bass

Servings:6
Cooking Time: 20 Minutes

Ingredients:

• ¼ teaspoon onion powder
• ¼ teaspoon garlic powder
• ¼ teaspoon paprika
• Lemon pepper and sea salt to taste
• 2 pounds sea bass
• 3 tablespoons extra-virgin olive oil, divided
• 2 large cloves garlic, chopped
• 1 tablespoon chopped Italian flat leaf parsley

Directions:

1. Preheat the grill to high heat.
2. Place the onion powder, garlic powder, paprika, lemon pepper, and sea salt in a large bowl and stir to combine.
3. Dredge the fish in the spice mixture, turning until well coated.
4. Heat 2 tablespoon of olive oil in a small skillet. Add the garlic and parsley and cook for 1 to 2 minutes, stirring occasionally. Remove the skillet from the heat and set aside.
5. Brush the grill grates lightly with remaining 1 tablespoon olive oil.
6. Grill the fish for about 7 minutes. Flip the fish and drizzle with the garlic mixture and cook for an additional 7 minutes, or until the fish flakes when pressed lightly with a fork.
7. Serve hot.

Nutrition Info:

• Info Per Serving: Calories: 200;Fat: 10.3g;Protein: 26.9g;Carbs: 0.6g.

Leek & Olive Cod Casserole

Servings:4
Cooking Time:30 Minutes

Ingredients:

• ½ cup olive oil
• 1 lb fresh cod fillets
• 1 cup black olives, chopped
• 4 leeks, trimmed and sliced
• 1 cup breadcrumbs
• ¾ cup chicken stock
• Salt and black pepper to taste

Directions:

1. Preheat oven to 350 F. Brush the cod with some olive oil, season with salt and pepper, and bake for 5-7 minutes. Let it cool, then cut it into 1-inch pieces.
2. Warm the remaining olive oil in a skillet over medium heat. Stir-fry the olives and leeks for 4 minutes

until the leeks are tender. Add the breadcrumbs and chicken stock, stirring to mix. Fold in the pieces of cod. Pour the mixture into a greased baking dish and bake for 15 minutes or until cooked through.

Nutrition Info:

- Info Per Serving: Calories: 534;Fat: 33g;Protein: 24g;Carbs: 36g.

Pancetta-wrapped Scallops

Servings:6
Cooking Time:25 Minutes

Ingredients:

- 2 tsp olive oil
- 12 thin pancetta slices
- 12 medium scallops
- 2 tsp lemon juice
- 1 tsp chili powder

Directions:

1. Wrap pancetta around scallops and secure with toothpicks. Warm the olive oil in a skillet over medium heat and cook scallops for 6 minutes on all sides. Serve sprinkled with chili powder and lemon juice.

Nutrition Info:

- Info Per Serving: Calories: 310;Fat: 25g;Protein: 19g;Carbs: 24g.

Simple Salmon With Balsamic Haricots Vert

Servings:4
Cooking Time:25 Minutes

Ingredients:

- 2 tbsp olive oil
- 3 tbsp balsamic vinegar
- 1 garlic clove, minced
- ½ tsp red pepper flakes
- 1 ½ lb haricots vert, chopped
- Salt and black pepper to taste
- 1 red onion, sliced
- 4 salmon fillets, boneless

Directions:

1. Warm half of oil in a skillet over medium heat and

sauté vinegar, onion, garlic, red pepper flakes, haricots vert, salt, and pepper for 6 minutes. Share into plates. Warm the remaining oil. Sprinkle salmon with salt and pepper and sear for 8 minutes on all sides. Serve with haricots vert.

Nutrition Info:

- Info Per Serving: Calories: 230;Fat: 16g;Protein: 17g;Carbs: 23g.

Thyme Hake With Potatoes

Servings:4
Cooking Time:40 Minutes

Ingredients:

- 1 ½ lb russet potatoes, unpeeled
- ¼ cup olive oil
- ½ tsp garlic powder
- ½ tsp paprika
- Salt and black pepper to taste
- 4 skinless hake fillets
- 4 fresh thyme sprigs
- 1 lemon, sliced

Directions:

1. Preheat oven to 425 F. Slice the potatoes and toss them with some olive oil, salt, pepper, paprika, and garlic powder in a bowl. Microwave for 12-14 minutes until potatoes are just tender, stirring halfway through microwaving.

2. Transfer the potatoes to a baking dish and press gently into an even layer. Season the hake with salt and pepper, and arrange it skinned side down over the potatoes. Drizzle with the remaining olive oil, then place thyme sprigs and lemon slices on top. Bake for 15-18 minutes until hake flakes apart when gently prodded with a paring knife. Serve and enjoy!

Nutrition Info:

- Info Per Serving: Calories: 410;Fat: 16g;Protein: 34g;Carbs: 33g.

Dill Chutney Salmon

Servings:2
Cooking Time: 3 Minutes

Ingredients:

- Chutney:
- ¼ cup fresh dill
- ¼ cup extra virgin olive oil
- Juice from ½ lemon
- Sea salt, to taste
- Fish:
- 2 cups water
- 2 salmon fillets
- Juice from ½ lemon
- ¼ teaspoon paprika
- Salt and freshly ground pepper to taste

Directions:

1. Pulse all the chutney ingredients in a food processor until creamy. Set aside.
2. Add the water and steamer basket to the Instant Pot. Place salmon fillets, skin-side down, on the steamer basket. Drizzle the lemon juice over salmon and sprinkle with the paprika.
3. Secure the lid. Select the Manual mode and set the cooking time for 3 minutes at High Pressure.
4. Once cooking is complete, do a quick pressure release. Carefully open the lid.
5. Season the fillets with pepper and salt to taste. Serve topped with the dill chutney.

Nutrition Info:

- Info Per Serving: Calories: 636;Fat: 41.1g;Protein: 65.3g;Carbs: 1.9g.

Crab Stuffed Celery Sticks

Servings:4
Cooking Time:10 Minutes

Ingredients:

- 1 cup cream cheese
- 6 oz crab meat
- 1 tsp Mediterranean seasoning
- 2 tbsp apple cider vinegar
- 8 celery sticks, halved
- Salt and black pepper to taste

Directions:

1. In a mixing bowl, combine the cream cheese, crab meat, apple cider vinegar, salt, pepper, and Mediterranean seasoning. Divide the crab mixture between the celery sticks. Serve.

Nutrition Info:

- Info Per Serving: Calories: 30;Fat: 2g;Protein: 3g;-Carbs: 1g.

Spicy Cod Fillets

Servings:4
Cooking Time:35 Minutes

Ingredients:

- 2 tbsp olive oil
- 1 tsp lime juice
- Salt and black pepper to taste
- 1 tsp sweet paprika
- 1 tsp chili powder
- 1 onion, chopped
- 2 garlic cloves, minced
- 4 cod fillets, boneless
- 1 tsp ground coriander
- ½ cup fish stock
- ½ lb cherry tomatoes, cubed

Directions:

1. Warm olive oil in a skillet over medium heat. Season the cod with salt, pepper, and chili powder and cook in the skillet for 8 minutes on all sides; set aside. In the same skillet, cook onion and garlic for 3 minutes. Stir in lime juice, paprika, coriander, fish stock, and cherry tomatoes and bring to a boil. Simmer for 10 minutes. Serve topped with cod fillets.

Nutrition Info:

- Info Per Serving: Calories: 240;Fat: 17g;Protein: 17g;Carbs: 26g.

Poultry And Meats Recipes

Easy Pork Souvlaki

Servings:6
Cooking Time:20 Min + Marinating Time

Ingredients:

- 3 tbsp olive oil
- 1 onion, grated
- 3 garlic cloves, minced
- 1 tsp ground cumin
- Salt and black pepper to taste
- 2 tsp dried oregano
- 2 lb boneless pork butt, cubed
- 2 lemons, cut into wedges

Directions:

1. In a large bowl, whisk the olive oil, onion, garlic, cumin, salt, pepper, and oregano. Add pork and toss to coat. Cover and place in the refrigerator for at least 2 hours or overnight.
2. Preheat your grill to medium-high. Thread the pork cubes onto bamboo skewers. Place the pork on the grill and cook for about 10 minutes on all sides or until the pork is cooked through. Serve with lemon wedges.

Nutrition Info:

- Info Per Serving: Calories: 279;Fat: 16g;Protein: 29g;Carbs: 5g.

Greek Peachy Lamb

Servings:4
Cooking Time:70 Minutes

Ingredients:

- 2 tbsp olive oil
- 1 lb lamb, cubed
- 2 cups Greek yogurt
- 2 peaches, peeled and cubed
- 1 onion, chopped
- 2 tbsp parsley, chopped
- ½ tsp red pepper flakes
- Salt and black pepper to taste

Directions:

1. Warm the olive oil in a skillet over medium heat and sear lamb for 5 minutes. Put in onion and cook for another 5 minutes. Stir in yogurt, peaches, parsley, red pepper flakes, salt, and pepper, and bring to a boil. Cook for 45 minutes.

Nutrition Info:

- Info Per Serving: Calories: 310;Fat: 16g;Protein: 16g;Carbs: 17g.

Marsala Chicken Cacciatore Stir-fry

Servings:4
Cooking Time:20 Minutes

Ingredients:

- 3 tbsp olive oil
- 1 lb chicken thigh strips
- ¼ cup Marsala white wine
- 1 tsp dried oregano
- Salt and black pepper to taste
- 2 tsp cornstarch
- 3 tbsp chicken broth
- 1 tomato, chopped
- 1 shallot, chopped
- 1 garlic clove, minced
- ¼ lb mushrooms, sliced
- 1 red bell pepper, sliced
- 2 fresh rosemary sprigs

Directions:

1. In a bowl, combine 2 tbsp of the wine, oregano, salt, pepper, and cornstarch. Add the chicken and toss to coat; set aside. Warm the olive oil in a skillet over medium heat and stir-fry the shallot and garlic for 1 minute until softened. Add the mushrooms and red bell pepper and sauté for 2-3 minutes until lightly tender. Remove to a plate.
2. Brown the chicken in the same skillet for about 5 minutes until it turns white and is nearly cooked through. Pour in the white wine, broth, and tomato

mixture while stir-frying. Bring to a boil. Add the vegetables back to the skillet. Cook, stirring, for another 2 minutes to mix everything together. Garnish with rosemary sprigs before serving.

Nutrition Info:

- Info Per Serving: Calories: 369;Fat: 29g;Protein: 20g;Carbs: 6g.

Chicken Caprese

Servings:4
Cooking Time:50 Minutes

Ingredients:

- 1 tsp garlic powder
- ½ cup basil pesto
- 4 chicken breast halves
- 3 tomatoes, sliced
- 1 cup mozzarella, shredded
- Salt and black pepper to taste

Directions:

1. Preheat the oven to 390 F. Line a baking dish with parchment paper and grease with cooking spray. Combine chicken, garlic powder, salt, pepper, and pesto in a bowl and arrange them on the sheet. Top with tomatoes and mozzarella and bake for 40 minutes. Serve hot.

Nutrition Info:

- Info Per Serving: Calories: 350;Fat: 21g;Protein: 33g;Carbs: 5g.

Chicken Cacciatore

Servings:2
Cooking Time: 1 Hour And 30 Minutes

Ingredients:

- 1½ pounds bone-in chicken thighs, skin removed and patted dry
- Salt, to taste
- 2 tablespoons olive oil
- ½ large onion, thinly sliced
- 4 ounces baby bella mushrooms, sliced
- 1 red sweet pepper, cut into 1-inch pieces
- 1 can crushed fire-roasted tomatoes
- 1 fresh rosemary sprig

- ½ cup dry red wine
- 1 teaspoon Italian herb seasoning
- ½ teaspoon garlic powder
- 3 tablespoons flour

Directions:

1. Season the chicken thighs with a generous pinch of salt.

2. Heat the olive oil in a Dutch oven over medium-high heat. Add the chicken and brown for 5 minutes per side.

3. Add the onion, mushrooms, and sweet pepper to the Dutch oven and sauté for another 5 minutes.

4. Add the tomatoes, rosemary, wine, Italian seasoning, garlic powder, and salt, stirring well.

5. Bring the mixture to a boil, then reduce the heat to low. Allow to simmer slowly for at least 1 hour, stirring occasionally, or until the chicken is tender and easily pulls away from the bone.

6. Measure out 1 cup of the sauce from the pot and put it into a bowl. Add the flour and whisk well to make a slurry.

7. Increase the heat to medium-high and slowly whisk the slurry into the pot. Stir until it comes to a boil and cook until the sauce is thickened.

8. Remove the chicken from the bones and shred it, and add it back to the sauce before serving, if desired.

Nutrition Info:

- Info Per Serving: Calories: 520;Fat: 23.1g;Protein: 31.8g;Carbs: 37.0g.

Cannellini Bean & Chicken Cassoulet

Servings:4
Cooking Time:40 Minutes

Ingredients:

- 1 lb chicken thighs, boneless and skinless
- 2 tbsp olive oil
- 2 tbsp tomato paste
- 1 celery stalk, chopped
- 1 sweet onion, chopped
- 2 garlic cloves, chopped
- ½ cup chicken stock
- 14 oz canned cannellini beans
- Salt and black pepper to taste

Directions:

1. Warm the olive oil in a pot over medium heat. Cook onion, celery, and garlic for 3 minutes. Put in chicken and cook for 6 minutes on all sides. Stir in tomato paste, stock, beans, salt, and pepper and bring to a boil. Cook for 30 minutes.

Nutrition Info:

• Info Per Serving: Calories: 260;Fat: 11g;Protein: 25g;Carbs: 26g.

Parmesan Chicken Breasts

Servings:4
Cooking Time:35 Minutes

Ingredients:

• 1 tbsp olive oil
• 1 ½ lb chicken breasts, cubed
• 1 tsp ground coriander
• 1 tsp parsley flakes
• 2 garlic cloves, minced
• 1 cup heavy cream
• Salt and black pepper to taste
• ¼ cup Parmesan cheese, grated
• 1 tbsp basil, chopped

Directions:

1. Warm the olive oil in a skillet over medium heat and brown chicken, salt, and pepper for 6 minutes on all sides. Add in garlic and cook for another minute. Stir in coriander, parsley, and cream and cook for an additional 20 minutes. Serve scattered with basil and Parmesan cheese.

Nutrition Info:

• Info Per Serving: Calories: 260;Fat: 18g;Protein: 27g;Carbs: 26g.

Rosemary Pork Loin With Green Onions

Servings:4
Cooking Time:50 Minutes

Ingredients:

• 2 lb pork loin roast, boneless and cubed
• 2 tbsp olive oil
• 2 garlic cloves, minced
• Salt and black pepper to taste
• 1 cup tomato sauce
• 1 tsp rosemary, chopped
• 4 green onions, chopped

Directions:

1. Preheat the oven to 360 F. Heat olive oil in a skillet over medium heat and cook pork, garlic, and green onions for 6-7 minutes, stirring often. Add in tomato sauce, rosemary, and 1 cup of water. Season with salt and pepper. Transfer to a baking dish and bake for 40 minutes. Serve warm.

Nutrition Info:

• Info Per Serving: Calories: 280;Fat: 16g;Protein: 19g;Carbs: 18g.

Bean & Chicken Cassoulet

Servings:4
Cooking Time:35 Minutes

Ingredients:

• 2 tbsp olive oil
• 4 chicken breast halves
• 1 onion, chopped
• 1 green bell pepper, chopped
• 2 garlic cloves, minced
• ½ cup Marsala wine
• 1 can diced tomatoes
• 1 can white beans
• 1 tbsp Italian seasoning
• 1 cup baby spinach
• ⅛ tsp red pepper flakes
• Salt and black pepper to taste

Directions:

1. Pound the chicken to ¾-inch thickness using a meat

mallet. Warm the olive oil in a pan over medium heat and brown the chicken for 6 minutes on both sides; set aside. In the same pan, sauté the onion, garlic, and bell pepper for 5 minutes.

2. Pour in the wine and scrape any bits from the bottom. Simmer for 1 minute. Stir in tomatoes, beans, Italian seasoning, salt, pepper, and pepper flakes. Bring just to a boil, then lower the heat and simmer for 5 minutes. Stir in spinach and put back the reserved chicken; cook for 3-4 more minutes. Serve.

Nutrition Info:

- Info Per Serving: Calories: 605;Fat: 12g;Protein: 48g;Carbs: 74g.

Beef Stuffed Peppers

Servings:4
Cooking Time:50 Minutes

Ingredients:

- 2 tbsp olive oil
- 2 red bell peppers
- 1 lb ground beef
- 1 shallot, finely chopped
- 2 garlic cloves, minced
- 2 tbsp fresh sage, chopped
- Salt and black pepper to taste
- 1 tsp ground allspice
- ½ cup fresh parsley, chopped
- ½ cup baby arugula leaves
- ½ cup pine nuts, chopped
- 1 tbsp orange juice

Directions:

1. Warm the olive oil in a large skillet over medium heat. Sauté the beef, garlic, and shallot for 8-10 minutes until the meat is browned and cooked through. Season with sage, allspice, salt, and pepper and remove from the heat to cool slightly. Stir in parsley, arugula, pine nuts, and orange juice and mix.

2. Preheat oven to 390 F. Slice the peppers in half lengthwise and remove the seeds and membranes. Spoon the filling into the pepper halves. Bake the oven for 25-30 minutes.

Nutrition Info:

- Info Per Serving: Calories: 521;Fat: 44g;Protein:

25g;Carbs: 9g.

Slow Cooker Beef Stew

Servings:4
Cooking Time:8 Hours 10 Minutes

Ingredients:

- 2 tbsp canola oil
- 2 lb beef stew meat, cubed
- Salt and black pepper to taste
- 2 cups beef stock
- 2 shallots, chopped
- 2 tbsp thyme, chopped
- 2 garlic cloves, minced
- 1 carrot, chopped
- 3 celery stalks, chopped
- 28 oz canned tomatoes, diced
- 2 tbsp parsley, chopped

Directions:

1. Place the beef meat, salt, pepper, beef stock, canola oil, shallots, thyme, garlic, carrot, celery, and tomatoes in your slow cooker. Put the lid and cook for 8 hours on Low. Sprinkle with parsley and serve warm.

Nutrition Info:

- Info Per Serving: Calories: 370;Fat: 17g;Protein: 35g;Carbs: 28g.

Saucy Turkey With Ricotta Cheese

Servings:4
Cooking Time:60 Minutes

Ingredients:

- 2 tbsp olive oil
- 1 turkey breast, cubed
- 1 ½ cups salsa verde
- Salt and black pepper to taste
- 4 oz ricotta cheese, crumbled
- 2 tbsp cilantro, chopped

Directions:

1. Preheat the oven to 380 F. Grease a roasting pan with oil. In a bowl, place turkey, salsa verde, salt, and pepper and toss to coat. Transfer to the roasting pan and bake for 50 minutes. Top with ricotta cheese and cilantro and serve.

Nutrition Info:

• Info Per Serving: Calories: 340;Fat: 16g;Protein: 35g;Carbs: 23g.

Crispy Pesto Chicken

Servings:2
Cooking Time: 50 Minutes

Ingredients:

• 12 ounces small red potatoes, scrubbed and diced into 1-inch pieces
• 1 tablespoon olive oil
• ½ teaspoon garlic powder
• ¼ teaspoon salt
• 1 boneless, skinless chicken breast
• 3 tablespoons prepared pesto

Directions:

1. Preheat the oven to 425ºF. Line a baking sheet with parchment paper.
2. Combine the potatoes, olive oil, garlic powder, and salt in a medium bowl. Toss well to coat.
3. Arrange the potatoes on the parchment paper and roast for 10 minutes. Flip the potatoes and roast for an additional 10 minutes.
4. Meanwhile, put the chicken in the same bowl and toss with the pesto, coating the chicken evenly.
5. Check the potatoes to make sure they are golden brown on the top and bottom. Toss them again and add the chicken breast to the pan.
6. Turn the heat down to 350ºF and roast the chicken and potatoes for 30 minutes. Check to make sure the chicken reaches an internal temperature of 165ºF and the potatoes are fork-tender.
7. Let cool for 5 minutes before serving.

Nutrition Info:

• Info Per Serving: Calories: 378;Fat: 16.0g;Protein: 29.8g;Carbs: 30.1g.

Lamb & Paprika Cannellini Beans

Servings:4
Cooking Time:50 Minutes

Ingredients:

• 1 can Cannellini beans
• 2 tbsp olive oil, divided
• 1 lb lamb shoulder, cubed
• Salt and black pepper to taste
• 2 garlic cloves, minced
• 1 large onion, diced
• 1 celery stalk, chopped
• 1 cup tomatoes, chopped
• 1 carrot, chopped
• ⅓ cup tomato paste
• 1 tsp paprika
• 1 tsp dried oregano

Directions:

1. Warm the olive oil in a pot over medium heat. Season the lamb with salt and pepper and sauté for 3-4 minutes until brown, stirring occasionally. Stir in the onion, celery, tomatoes, and carrots and cook for 4-5 minutes.
2. Add the paprika and tomato paste and stir to combine. Pour in the beans and 2 cups water. Bring the mixture to a boil and simmer for 20-25 minutes until the lamb is cooked. Season with salt, pepper, and oregano and serve.

Nutrition Info:

• Info Per Serving: Calories: 520;Fat: 24g;Protein: 37g;Carbs: 42g.

Cranberry Turkey Bake

Servings:4
Cooking Time:40 Minutes

Ingredients:

• 2 tbsp canola oil
• 1 turkey breast, sliced
• 1 cup chicken stock
• ½ cup cranberry sauce
• ½ cup orange juice
• 1 tsp mustard powder
• 1 onion, chopped

- Salt and black pepper to taste

Directions:

1. Warm canola oil in a saucepan over medium heat. Cook onion for 3 minutes. Put in turkey and cook for another 5 minutes, turning once. Season with mustard powder, salt, and pepper. Pour in the cranberry sauce, chicken stock, and orange juice and bring to a boil; simmer for 20 minutes.

Nutrition Info:

- Info Per Serving: Calories: 390;Fat: 14g;Protein: 19g;Carbs: 28g.

Panko Grilled Chicken Patties

Servings:4
Cooking Time: 8 To 10 Minutes

Ingredients:

- 1 pound ground chicken
- 3 tablespoons crumbled feta cheese
- 3 tablespoons finely chopped red pepper
- ¼ cup finely chopped red onion
- 3 tablespoons panko bread crumbs
- 1 garlic clove, minced
- 1 teaspoon chopped fresh oregano
- ¼ teaspoon salt
- ⅛ teaspoon freshly ground black pepper
- Cooking spray

Directions:

1. Mix together the ground chicken, feta cheese, red pepper, red onion, bread crumbs, garlic, oregano, salt, and black pepper in a large bowl, and stir to incorporate.
2. Divide the chicken mixture into 8 equal portions and form each portion into a patty with your hands.
3. Preheat a grill to medium-high heat and oil the grill grates with cooking spray.
4. Arrange the patties on the grill grates and grill each side for 4 to 5 minutes, or until the patties are cooked through.
5. Rest for 5 minutes before serving.

Nutrition Info:

- Info Per Serving: Calories: 241;Fat: 13.5g;Protein: 23.2g;Carbs: 6.7g.

Grilled Lemon Chicken

Servings:2
Cooking Time: 12 To 14 Minutes

Ingredients:

- Marinade:
- 4 tablespoons freshly squeezed lemon juice
- 2 tablespoons olive oil, plus more for greasing the grill grates
- 1 teaspoon dried basil
- 1 teaspoon paprika
- ½ teaspoon dried thyme
- ¼ teaspoon salt
- ¼ teaspoon garlic powder
- 2 boneless, skinless chicken breasts

Directions:

1. Make the marinade: Whisk together the lemon juice, olive oil, basil, paprika, thyme, salt, and garlic powder in a large bowl until well combined.
2. Add the chicken breasts to the bowl and let marinate for at least 30 minutes.
3. When ready to cook, preheat the grill to medium-high heat. Lightly grease the grill grates with the olive oil.
4. Discard the marinade and arrange the chicken breasts on the grill grates.
5. Grill for 12 to 14 minutes, flipping the chicken halfway through, or until a meat thermometer inserted in the center of the chicken reaches 165ºF.
6. Let the chicken cool for 5 minutes and serve warm.

Nutrition Info:

- Info Per Serving: Calories: 251;Fat: 15.5g;Protein: 27.3g;Carbs: 1.9g.

Spinach-ricotta Chicken Rolls

Servings:4
Cooking Time:55 Minutes

Ingredients:

2 tbsp olive oil
4 chicken breast halves
1 lb baby spinach
2 garlic cloves, minced
1 lemon, zested
½ cup crumbled ricotta cheese
1 tbsp pine nuts, toasted
Salt and black pepper to taste

Directions:

1. Preheat oven to 350 F. Pound the chicken breasts to ½-inch thickness with a meat mallet and season with salt and pepper.

2. Warm olive oil in a pan over medium heat and sauté spinach for 4-5 minutes until it wilts. Stir in garlic, salt, lemon zest, and pepper for 20-30 seconds. Let cool slightly and add in ricotta cheese and pine nuts; mix well. Spoon the mixture over the chicken breasts, wrap around the filling, and secure the ends with toothpicks. Arrange the breasts on a greased baking dish and bake for 35-40 minutes. Let sit for a few minutes and slice. Serve immediately.

Nutrition Info:

• Info Per Serving: Calories: 260;Fat: 14g;Protein: 8g;Carbs: 6.5g.

Chicken Drumsticks With Peach Glaze

Servings:4
Cooking Time:35 Minutes

Ingredients:

2 tbsp olive oil
8 chicken drumsticks, skinless
3 peaches, peeled and chopped
¼ cup honey
¼ cup cider vinegar
1 sweet onion, chopped
1 tsp minced fresh rosemary
Salt to taste

Directions:

1. Warm the olive oil in a large skillet over medium heat. Sprinkle chicken with salt and pepper and brown it for about 7 minutes per side. Remove to a plate. Add onion and rosemary to the skillet and sauté for 1 minute or until lightly golden. Add honey, vinegar, salt, and peaches and cook for 10-12 minutes or until peaches are softened. Add the chicken back to the skillet and heat just until warm, brushing with the sauce. Serve chicken thighs with peach sauce. Enjoy!

Nutrition Info:

• Info Per Serving: Calories: 1492;Fat: 26g;Protein: 54g;Carbs: 27g.

Harissa Beef Burgers

Servings:2
Cooking Time:30 Minutes

Ingredients:

• ½ small onion, minced
• 1 garlic clove, minced
• 1 tsp fresh rosemary, chopped
• Salt and black pepper to taste
• 1 tsp cumin
• 1 tsp smoked paprika
• ¼ tsp ground coriander
• ¼ tsp dried oregano
• 8 oz ground beef
• 2 tbsp olive oil
• 1 cup yogurt
• ½ tsp harissa paste

Directions:

1. Preheat your grill to 350 F. In a bowl, combine the ground beef, onion, garlic, rosemary, salt, pepper, cumin, paprika, oregano, and coriander until is well incorporated. Form the mixture into 2 patties using your hands. Grill the burgers for 6-8 minutes on all sides. Whisk the yogurt and harissa in a small bowl. Serve the burgers with harissa yogurt.

Nutrition Info:

• Info Per Serving: Calories: 381;Fat: 20g;Protein: 22g;Carbs: 27g.

Baked Garlicky Pork Chops

Servings:4
Cooking Time:45 Minutes

Ingredients:

- 1 tbsp olive oil
- 4 pork loin chops, boneless
- Salt and black pepper to taste
- 4 garlic cloves, minced
- 1 tbsp thyme, chopped

Directions:

1. Preheat the oven to 390 F. Place pork chops, salt, pepper, garlic, thyme, and olive oil in a roasting pan and bake for 10 minutes. Decrease the heat to 360 F and bake for 25 minutes.

Nutrition Info:

- Info Per Serving: Calories: 170;Fat: 6g;Protein: 26g;Carbs: 2g.

Parsley-dijon Chicken And Potatoes

Servings:6
Cooking Time: 22 Minutes

Ingredients:

- 1 tablespoon extra-virgin olive oil
- 1½ pounds boneless, skinless chicken thighs, cut into 1-inch cubes, patted dry
- 1½ pounds Yukon Gold potatoes, unpeeled, cut into ½-inch cubes
- 2 garlic cloves, minced
- ¼ cup dry white wine
- 1 cup low-sodium or no-salt-added chicken broth
- 1 tablespoon Dijon mustard
- ¼ teaspoon freshly ground black pepper
- ¼ teaspoon kosher or sea salt
- 1 cup chopped fresh flat-leaf (Italian) parsley, including stems
- 1 tablespoon freshly squeezed lemon juice

Directions:

1. In a large skillet over medium-high heat, heat the oil. Add the chicken and cook for 5 minutes, stirring only after the chicken has browned on one side. Remove the chicken and reserve on a plate.

2. Add the potatoes to the skillet and cook for 5 minutes, stirring only after the potatoes have become golden and crispy on one side. Push the potatoes to the side of the skillet, add the garlic, and cook, stirring constantly, for 1 minute. Add the wine and cook for 1 minute, until nearly evaporated. Add the chicken broth, mustard, salt, pepper, and reserved chicken. Turn the heat to high and bring to a boil.

3. Once boiling, cover, reduce the heat to medium-low, and cook for 10 to 12 minutes, until the potatoes are tender and the internal temperature of the chicken measures 165ºF on a meat thermometer and any juices run clear.

4. During the last minute of cooking, stir in the parsley. Remove from the heat, stir in the lemon juice, and serve.

Nutrition Info:

- Info Per Serving: Calories: 324;Fat: 9.0g;Protein: 16.0g;Carbs: 45.0g.

Sweet Pork Stew

Servings:4
Cooking Time:50 Minutes

Ingredients:

- 3 tbsp olive oil
- 1 ½ lb pork stew meat, cubed
- Salt and black pepper to taste
- 1 cup red onions, chopped
- 1 cup dried apricots, chopped
- 2 garlic cloves, minced
- 1 cup canned tomatoes, diced
- 2 tbsp parsley, chopped

Directions:

1. Warm olive oil in a skillet over medium heat. Sear pork meat for 5 minutes. Put in onions and cook for another 5 minutes. Stir in salt, pepper, apricots, garlic, tomatoes, and parsley and bring to a simmer and cook for an additional 30 minutes.

Nutrition Info:

- Info Per Serving: Calories: 320;Fat: 17g;Protein: 35g;Carbs: 22g.

Spicy Beef Zoodles

Servings:4
Cooking Time:20 Minutes

Ingredients:

- 2 tbsp olive oil
- 1 lb beef steaks, sliced
- 2 zucchinis, spiralized
- ½ cup sweet chili sauce
- 1 cup carrot, grated
- 3 tbsp water
- Salt and black pepper to taste

Directions:

1. Warm the olive oil in a skillet over medium heat and brown beef steaks for 8 minutes on both side; reserve and cover with foil to keep warm. Stir zucchini noodles, chili sauce, carrot, water, salt, and pepper and cook for an additional 3-4 minutes. Remove the foil from the steaks and pour the zucchini mix over to serve.

Nutrition Info:

- Info Per Serving: Calories: 360;Fat: 12g;Protein: 37g;Carbs: 26g.

Chicken Gyros With Tzatziki Sauce

Servings:2
Cooking Time: 10 Minutes

Ingredients:

- 2 tablespoons freshly squeezed lemon juice
- 2 tablespoons olive oil, divided, plus more for oiling the grill
- 1 teaspoon minced fresh oregano
- ½ teaspoon garlic powder
- Salt, to taste
- 8 ounces chicken tenders
- 1 small eggplant, cut into 1-inch strips lengthwise
- 1 small zucchini, cut into ½-inch strips lengthwise
- ½ red pepper, seeded and cut in half lengthwise
- ½ English cucumber, peeled and minced
- ¾ cup plain Greek yogurt
- 1 tablespoon minced fresh dill
- 2 pita breads

Directions:

1. Combine the lemon juice, 1 tablespoon of olive oil, oregano, garlic powder, and salt in a medium bowl. Add the chicken and let marinate for 30 minutes.
2. Place the eggplant, zucchini, and red pepper in a large mixing bowl and sprinkle with salt and the remaining 1 tablespoon of olive oil. Toss well to coat. Let the vegetables rest while the chicken is marinating.
3. Make the tzatziki sauce: Combine the cucumber, yogurt, salt, and dill in a medium bowl. Stir well to incorporate and set aside in the refrigerator.
4. When ready, preheat the grill to medium-high heat and oil the grill grates.
5. Drain any liquid from the vegetables and put them on the grill.
6. Remove the chicken tenders from the marinade and put them on the grill.
7. Grill the chicken and vegetables for 3 minutes per side, or until the chicken is no longer pink inside.
8. Remove the chicken and vegetables from the grill and set aside. On the grill, heat the pitas for about 30 seconds, flipping them frequently.
9. Divide the chicken tenders and vegetables between the pitas and top each with ¼ cup of the prepared sauce. Roll the pitas up like a cone and serve.

Nutrition Info:

- Info Per Serving: Calories: 586;Fat: 21.9g;Protein: 39.0g;Carbs: 62.0g.

Grilled Pork Chops With Apricot Chutney

Servings:4
Cooking Time:40 Minutes

Ingredients:

- 1 tbsp olive oil
- ½ tsp garlic powder
- 4 pork loin chops, boneless
- Salt and black pepper to taste
- ¼ tsp ground cumin
- ½ tsp sage, dried
- 1 tsp chili powder
- For the chutney
- 3 cups apricots, peeled and chopped
- ½ cup red sweet pepper, chopped
- 1 tsp olive oil

- ¼ cup shallot, minced
- ½ jalapeno pepper, minced
- 1 tbsp balsamic vinegar
- 2 tbsp cilantro, chopped

Directions:

1. Warm the olive oil in a skillet over medium heat and cook the shallot for 5 minutes. Stir in sweet pepper, apricots, jalapeño pepper, vinegar, and cilantro and cook for 10 minutes. Remove from heat.

2. In the meantime, sprinkle pork chops with olive oil, salt, pepper, garlic powder, cumin, sage, and chili powder. Preheat the grill to medium heat. Grill pork chops for 12-14 minutes on both sides. Serve topped with apricot chutney.

Nutrition Info:

- Info Per Serving: Calories: 300;Fat: 11g;Protein: 39g;Carbs: 14g.

Herby Turkey Stew

Servings:4
Cooking Time:60 Minutes

Ingredients:

- 1 skinless, boneless turkey breast, cubed
- 2 tbsp olive oil
- Salt and black pepper to taste
- 1 tbsp sweet paprika
- ½ cup chicken stock
- 1 lb pearl onions
- 2 garlic cloves, minced
- 1 carrot, sliced
- 1 tsp cumin, ground
- 1 tbsp basil, chopped
- 1 tbsp cilantro, chopped

Directions:

1. Warm the olive oil in a pot over medium heat and sear turkey for 8 minutes, stirring occasionally. Stir in pearl onions, carrot, and garlic and cook for another 3 minutes. Season with salt, pepper, cumin, and paprika. Pour in the stock and bring to a boil; cook for 40 minutes. Top with basil and cilantro.

Nutrition Info:

- Info Per Serving: Calories: 260;Fat: 12g;Protein:

19g;Carbs: 24g.

Mustardy Turkey Ham Stuffed Peppers

Servings:4
Cooking Time:10 Minutes

Ingredients:

- 1 cup Greek yogurt
- 1 lb turkey ham, chopped
- 2 tbsp mustard
- Salt and black pepper to taste
- 1 celery stalk, chopped
- 2 tbsp balsamic vinegar
- 1 bunch scallions, sliced
- ¼ cup parsley, chopped
- 1 cucumber, sliced
- 1 red bell peppers, halved and deseeded
- 1 tomato, sliced

Directions:

1. Preheat the oven to 360 F. Combine turkey ham, celery, balsamic vinegar, salt, pepper, mustard, yogurt, scallions, parsley, cucumber, and tomatoes in a bowl. Fill bell peppers with the mixture and arrange them on a greased baking dish. Bake in the oven for about 20 minutes. Serve warm.

Nutrition Info:

- Info Per Serving: Calories: 280;Fat: 13g;Protein: 4g;Carbs: 16g.

Bell Pepper & Onion Pork Chops

Servings:4
Cooking Time:30 Minutes

Ingredients:

- 2 tbsp olive oil
- 4 pork chops
- Salt and black pepper to taste
- 1 tsp fennel seeds
- 1 red bell pepper, sliced
- 1 green bell pepper, sliced
- 1 yellow onion, thinly sliced
- 2 tsp Italian seasoning
- 2 garlic cloves, minced
- 1 tbsp balsamic vinegar

Directions:

1. Warm the olive oil in a large skillet over medium heat. Season the pork chops with salt and pepper and add them to the skillet. Cook for 6-8 minutes on both sides or until golden brown; reserve. Sauté the garlic, sliced bell peppers, onions, fennel seeds, and herbs in the skillet for 6-8 minutes until tender, stirring occasionally. Return the pork, cover, and lower the heat to low. Cook for another 3 minutes or until the pork is cooked through. Transfer the pork and vegetables to a serving platter. Add the vinegar to the skillet and stir to combine for 1-2 minutes. Drizzle the sauce over the pork.

Nutrition Info:

- Info Per Serving: Calories: 508;Fat: 40g;Protein: 31g;Carbs: 8g.

Chicken With Chianti Sauce

Servings:4
Cooking Time:80 Min + Chilling Time

Ingredients:

- 4 tbsp olive oil
- 2 tbsp butter
- 3 garlic cloves, minced
- 1 tbsp lemon zest
- 2 tbsp fresh thyme, chopped
- 2 tbsp fresh parsley, chopped
- Salt and black pepper to taste
- 4 bone-in chicken legs
- 2 cups red grapes (in clusters)
- 1 red onion, sliced
- 1 cup Chianti red wine
- 1 cup chicken stock

Directions:

1. Toss the chicken with 2 tbsp of olive oil, garlic, thyme, parsley, lemon zest, salt, and pepper in a bowl. Refrigerate for 1 hour. Preheat oven to 400 F. Heat the remaining olive oil in a saucepan over medium heat. Sear the chicken for 3–4 minutes per side. Top chicken with the grapes. Transfer to the oven and bake for 20–30 minutes or until internal temperature registers 180 F on an instant-read thermometer.

2. Melt the butter in another saucepan and sauté the onion for 3–4 minutes. Add the wine and stock, stir, and simmer the sauce for about 30 minutes until it is thickened. Plate the chicken and grapes and pour the sauce over to serve.

Nutrition Info:

- Info Per Serving: Calories: 562;Fat: 31g;Protein: 52g;Carbs: 16g.

Sides , Salads, And Soups Recipes

Feta Topped Zucchini Pancakes

Servings:4
Cooking Time:20 Minutes

Ingredients:

- 1 cup feta cheese, crumbled
- 1 cup flour
- ½ tsp baking powder
- ½ tsp dried oregano
- ½ tsp dried basil
- ½ tsp dried rosemary
- Salt and black pepper to taste
- 1 ½ cups zucchini, grated
- 1 egg
- ½ cup rice milk
- 1 tsp garlic, minced
- 2 tbsp scallions, sliced
- 4 tbsp olive oil

Directions:

1. In a bowl, thoroughly combine the flour, baking powder, and spices. In a separate bowl, combine the zucchini, egg, milk, garlic, and scallions. Add the zucchini mixture to the dry flour mixture and stir to combine well. Warm the olive oil in a pan over medium heat. Cook each pancake for 2-3 minutes per side until golden brown. Serve topped with feta cheese.

Nutrition Info:

- Info Per Serving: Calories: 262;Fat: 14g;Protein: 5g;Carbs: 27g.

Chicken & Mushroom Soup

Servings:4
Cooking Time:30 Minutes

Ingredients:

- 2 tbsp olive oil
- 1 can diced tomatoes
- ½ lb chicken breasts, cubed
- 4 cups chicken broth

- 2 carrots, chopped
- 1 onion, chopped
- 1 red bell pepper, chopped
- 1 fennel bulb, chopped
- 2 garlic cloves, minced
- ½ tsp paprika
- 1 cup mushrooms, sliced
- 1 tbsp Italian seasoning
- Salt and black pepper to taste

Directions:

1. Warm the olive oil in a pot over medium heat. Place in chicken and brown for 5 minutes. Set aside.

2. Add in onion, carrots, bell pepper, and fennel, sauté for 5 minutes until softened. Throw in garlic and paprika and cook for 30 seconds. Mix in tomatoes, mushrooms, Italian seasoning, broth, chicken, salt, and pepper. Bring to a boil, then decrease the heat and simmer for 20 minutes. Serve.

Nutrition Info:

- Info Per Serving: Calories: 293;Fat: 14g;Protein: 24g;Carbs: 19g.

Restaurant-style Zuppa Di Fagioli

Servings:4
Cooking Time:10 Minutes

Ingredients:

- 2 tbsp Pecorino cheese, grated
- 2 tbsp olive oil
- 1 carrot, peeled and diced
- 1 onion, chopped
- 2 cloves garlic, chopped
- 4 cups chicken broth
- ½ cup white beans, soaked
- 1 tsp dried thyme
- Salt and black pepper to taste
- 4 whole-wheat bread slices

Directions:

1. Warm the olive oil in a large stockpot over medium heat. Add the carrot and onion and sauté until the onion is translucent. Stir-fry the garlic for 1 more minute. Pour in the broth, beans, salt, and pepper, and cover. Bring to a boil and simmer for 2 hours or until the beans are tender. Adjust the taste and top with Pecorino cheese. Serve with toasted whole-wheat bread.

Nutrition Info:

• Info Per Serving: Calories: 186;Fat: 3g;Protein: 6g;-Carbs: 24g.

Minty Lamb Egg Soup

Servings:4
Cooking Time:50 Minutes

Ingredients:

• 2 tbsp olive oil
• ½ lb lamb meat, cubed
• 3 eggs, whisked
• 4 cups beef broth
• 5 spring onions, chopped
• 2 tbsp mint, chopped
• 2 lemons, juiced
• Salt and black pepper to taste
• 1 cup baby spinach

Directions:

1. Warm the olive oil in a pot over medium heat and cook lamb for 10 minutes, stirring occasionally. Add in spring onions and cook for another 3 minutes. Pour in beef broth, salt, and pepper and simmer for 30 minutes. Whisk eggs with lemon juice and some soup, pour into the pot, and spinach and cook for an additional 5 minutes. Sprinkle with mint and serve.

Nutrition Info:

• Info Per Serving: Calories: 290;Fat: 29g;Protein: 6g;Carbs: 3g.

Yogurt Cucumber Salad

Servings:4
Cooking Time:10 Min + Chilling Time

Ingredients:

• 1 tbsp olive oil
• 2 tbsp walnuts, ground
• 1 cup Greek yogurt
• 2 garlic cloves, minced
• Salt and white pepper to taste
• 1 tbsp wine vinegar
• 1 tbsp dill, chopped
• 3 medium cucumbers, sliced
• 1 tbsp chives, chopped

Directions:

1. Combine cucumbers, walnuts, garlic, salt, pepper, vinegar, yogurt, dill, olive oil, and chives in a bowl. Let sit in the fridge for 1 hour. Serve.

Nutrition Info:

• Info Per Serving: Calories: 220;Fat: 13g;Protein: 4g;Carbs: 9g.

Rice Stuffed Bell Peppers

Servings:4
Cooking Time:70 Minutes

Ingredients:

• 4 red bell peppers, tops and seeds removed
• 2 tbsp olive oil
• 1 cup cooked brown rice
• 4 oz crumbled feta cheese
• 4 cups fresh baby spinach
• 3 Roma tomatoes, chopped
• 1 onion, finely chopped
• 1 cup mushrooms, sliced
• 2 garlic cloves, minced
• 1 tsp dried oregano
• Salt and black pepper to taste
• 2 tbsp fresh parsley, chopped

Directions:

1. Preheat oven to 350 F. Warm olive oil in a skillet over medium heat and sauté onion, garlic, and mushrooms for 5 minutes. Stir in tomatoes, spinach, rice

salt, oregano, parsley, and pepper, cook for 3 minutes until the spinach wilts. Remove from the heat. Stuff the bell peppers with the rice mixture and top with feta cheese. Arrange the peppers on a greased baking pan and pour in 1/4 cup of water. Bake covered with aluminum foil for 30 minutes. Then, bake uncovered for another 10 minutes. Serve and enjoy!

Nutrition Info:

• Info Per Serving: Calories: 387;Fat: 15g;Protein: 12g;Carbs: 55g.

Creamy Roasted Red Pepper Soup With Feta

Servings:6
Cooking Time:30 Minutes

Ingredients:

• 8 roasted red peppers, chopped
• 2 roasted chili peppers, chopped
• 3 tbsp olive oil
• 2 shallots, chopped
• 4 garlic cloves, minced
• 2 tsp chopped fresh oregano
• 6 cups chicken broth
• Salt and black pepper to taste
• ¼ cup heavy cream
• 1 lemon, juiced
• ½ cup feta cheese, crumbled

Directions:

1. Puree all of the roasted peppers in your food processor until smooth. Warm the olive oil in a pot over medium heat and add the shallots and garlic. Cook until soft and translucent, about 5 minutes. Add the pepper mixture and oregano, followed by the broth. Bring to a boil on high heat and sprinkle with salt and pepper. Lower the heat to low and simmer for 15 minutes. Stir in the heavy cream and lemon juice. Ladle into individual bowls and garnish with feta. Serve immediately.

Nutrition Info:

Info Per Serving: Calories: 223;Fat: 6g;Protein: 1g;Carbs: 31g.

Orange Pear Salad With Gorgonzola

Servings:4
Cooking Time:10 Minutes

Ingredients:

• 4 oz gorgonzola cheese, crumbled
• 2 tbsp olive oil
• 1 tsp orange zest
• ¼ cup orange juice
• 3 tbsp balsamic vinegar
• Salt and black pepper to taste
• 1 romaine lettuce head, torn
• 2 pears, cored and cut into medium wedges

Directions:

1. Mix orange zest, orange juice, vinegar, oil, salt, pepper, lettuce, pears, and gorgonzola cheese in a bowl. Serve.

Nutrition Info:

• Info Per Serving: Calories: 210;Fat: 6g;Protein: 4g;-Carbs: 11g.

Gorgonzola, Fig & Prosciutto Salad

Servings:2
Cooking Time:15 Minutes

Ingredients:

• 2 tbsp crumbled Gorgonzola cheese
• 2 tbsp olive oil
• 3 cups Romaine lettuce, torn
• 4 figs, sliced
• 3 thin prosciutto slices
• ¼ cup pecan halves, toasted
• 1 tbsp balsamic vinegar

Directions:

1. Toss lettuce and figs in a large bowl. Drizzle with olive oil. Slice the prosciutto lengthwise into 1-inch strips. Add the prosciutto, pecans, and Gorgonzola cheese to the bowl. Toss the salad lightly. Drizzle with balsamic vinegar.

Nutrition Info:

• Info Per Serving: Calories: 519;Fat: 38g;Protein: 20g;Carbs: 29g.

Parmesan Chicken Salad

Servings:4
Cooking Time:15 Minutes

Ingredients:

- 2 cups chopped cooked chicken breasts
- 1 cup canned artichoke hearts, chopped
- 2 tbsp extra-virgin olive oil
- 2 tomatoes, chopped
- 2 heads romaine lettuce, torn
- 2 cucumbers, chopped
- ½ red onion, finely chopped
- 3 oz Parmesan cheese, shaved
- 4 oz pesto
- 1 lemon, zested
- 2 garlic cloves, minced
- 2 tbsp chopped fresh basil
- 2 tbsp chopped scallions
- Salt and black pepper to taste

Directions:

1. Mix the lettuce, artichoke, chicken, tomatoes, cucumbers, and red onion in a bowl. In another bowl, mix pesto, olive oil, lemon zest, garlic, basil, salt, and pepper and stir to combine. Drizzle the pesto dressing over the salad and top with scallions and Parmesan cheese shavings to serve.

Nutrition Info:

- Info Per Serving: Calories: 461;Fat: 29g;Protein: 33g;Carbs: 19g.

Pecorino Zucchini Strips

Servings:4
Cooking Time:30 Minutes

Ingredients:

- 4 zucchini, quartered lengthwise
- 2 tbsp olive oil
- ½ cup grated Pecorino cheese
- 1 tbsp dried dill
- ¼ tsp garlic powder
- Salt and black pepper to taste

Directions:

1. Preheat oven to 350 F. Combine zucchini and olive oil in a bowl. Mix cheese, salt, garlic powder, dill, and pepper in a bowl. Add in zucchini and toss to combine. Arrange the zucchini fingers on a lined baking sheet and bake for about 20 minutes until golden Set oven to broil and broil for 2 minutes until crispy. Serve and enjoy!

Nutrition Info:

- Info Per Serving: Calories: 103;Fat: 8.2g;Protein: 3.5g;Carbs: 6g.

Roasted Red Pepper & Olive Spread

Servings:6
Cooking Time:10 Minutes

Ingredients:

- ¼ tsp dried thyme
- 1 tbsp capers
- ½ cup pitted green olives
- 1 roasted red pepper, chopped
- 1 tsp balsamic vinegar
- 2/3 cup soft bread crumbs
- 2 cloves garlic, minced
- ½ tsp red pepper flakes
- 1/3 cup extra-virgin olive oil

Directions:

1. Place all the ingredients, except for the olive oil, in a food processor and blend until chunky. With the machine running, slowly pour in the olive oil until it is well combined. Refrigerate or serve at room temperature.

Nutrition Info:

- Info Per Serving: Calories: 467;Fat: 38g;Protein: 5g;Carbs: 27g.

Olive Tapenade Flatbread With Cheese

Servings:4
Cooking Time:35 Min + Chilling Time

Ingredients:

- For the flatbread
- 2 tbsp olive oil
- 2 ½ tsp dry yeast
- 1 ½ cups all-purpose flour
- ¾ tsp salt
- ½ cup lukewarm water
- ¼ tsp sugar
- For the tapenade
- 2 roasted red pepper slices, chopped
- ¼ cup extra-virgin olive oil
- 1 cup green olives, chopped
- 10 black olives, chopped
- 1 tbsp capers
- 1 garlic clove, minced
- 1 tbsp chopped basil leaves
- 1 tbsp chopped fresh oregano
- ¼ cup goat cheese, crumbled

Directions:

1. Combine lukewarm water, sugar, and yeast in a bowl. Set aside covered for 5 minutes. Mix the flour and salt in a bowl. Pour in the yeast mixture and mix. Knead until you obtain a ball. Place the dough onto a floured surface and knead for 5 minutes until soft. Leave the dough into an oiled bowl, covered to rise until it has doubled in size, about 40 minutes.
2. Preheat oven to 400 F. Cut the dough into 4 balls and roll each one out to a ½ inch thickness. Bake for 5 minutes. In a blender, mix black olives, roasted pepper, green olives, capers, garlic, oregano, basil, and olive oil for 20 seconds until coarsely chopped. Spread the olive tapenade on the flatbreads and top with goat cheese to serve.

Nutrition Info:

- Info Per Serving: Calories: 366;Fat: 19g;Protein: 7.3g;Carbs: 42g.

Cucumber Salad With Goat Cheese

Servings:4
Cooking Time:15 Minutes

Ingredients:

- 2 tbsp olive oil
- 4 oz goat cheese, crumbled
- 2 cucumbers, sliced
- 2 spring onions, chopped
- 2 garlic cloves, grated
- Salt and black pepper to taste

Directions:

1. Combine cucumbers, spring onions, olive oil, garlic, salt, pepper, and goat cheese in a bowl. Serve chilled.

Nutrition Info:

- Info Per Serving: Calories: 150;Fat: 6g;Protein: 6g;Carbs: 8g.

Kalamata Olive & Lentil Salad

Servings:4
Cooking Time:25 Min + Chilling Time

Ingredients:

- 1 cup red lentils, rinsed
- 1 tsp yellow mustard
- ½ lemon, juiced
- 2 tbsp tamari sauce
- 2 scallion stalks, chopped
- ¼ cup extra-virgin olive oil
- 2 garlic cloves, minced
- 1 cup butterhead lettuce, torn
- 2 tbsp fresh parsley, chopped
- 2 tbsp fresh cilantro, chopped
- 1 tsp fresh basil
- 1 tsp fresh oregano
- 12 cherry tomatoes, halved
- 6 Kalamata olives, halved

Directions:

1. Pour 5 cups of salted water and lentils in a large pot over high heat and bring to a boil. Reduce the heat to medium-low and simmer for 15-18 minutes until the lentils are tender. Drain and let it cool completely.

Transfer them to a salad bowl and add in the remaining ingredients, except for the olives; toss until well combined. Top with olives and serve.

Nutrition Info:

• Info Per Serving: Calories: 348;Fat: 16g;Protein: 16g;Carbs: 41g.

Zoodles With Tomato-mushroom Sauce

Servings:4
Cooking Time:25 Minutes

Ingredients:

• 1 lb oyster mushrooms, chopped
• 2 tbsp olive oil
• 1 cup chicken broth
• 1 tsp Mediterranean sauce
• 1 yellow onion, minced
• 1 cup pureed tomatoes
• 2 garlic cloves, minced
• 2 zucchinis, spiralized

Directions:

1. Warm the olive oil in a saucepan over medium heat and sauté the zoodles for 1-2 minutes; reserve. Sauté the onion and garlic in the same saucepan for 2-3 minutes. Add in the mushrooms and continue to cook for 2 to 3 minutes until they release liquid. Add in the remaining ingredients and cover the pan; let it simmer for 10 minutes longer until everything is cooked through. Top the zoodles with the prepared mushroom sauce and serve.

Nutrition Info:

• Info Per Serving: Calories: 95;Fat: 6.4g;Protein: 6g;-Carbs: 5g.

Roasted Pepper & Tomato Soup

Servings:4
Cooking Time:30 Minutes

Ingredients:

• 1 cup roasted bell peppers, chopped
• 2 tbsp olive oil
• 3 tomatoes, cored and halved
• 2 cloves garlic, minced
• 1 yellow onion, quartered
• 1 celery stalk, chopped
• 1 carrot, shredded
• ½ tsp ground cumin
• ½ tsp chili pepper
• 4 cups vegetable broth
• ½ tsp red pepper flakes
• 2 tbsp fresh basil, chopped
• Salt and black pepper to taste
• ¼ cup crème fraîche

Directions:

1. Heat oven to 380 F. Arrange the tomatoes and peppers on a roasting pan. Drizzle olive oil over the vegetables. Roast for 20 minutes until charred. Remove, let cool, and peel them.
2. Heat olive oil in a pot over medium heat and sauté onion, garlic, celery, and carrots for 3-5 minutes until tender. Stir in chili pepper and cumin for 1-2 minutes.
3. Pour in roasted bell peppers and tomatoes, stir, then add in the vegetable broth. Season with salt and pepper. Bring to a boil and reduce the heat; simmer for 10 minutes. Using an immersion blender, purée the soup until smooth. Sprinkle with pepper flakes and basil. Serve topped with crème fraîche.

Nutrition Info:

• Info Per Serving: Calories: 164;Fat: 12g;Protein: 6.5g;Carbs: 9.8g.

Homemade Herbes De Provence Spice

Servings:4
Cooking Time:5 Minutes

Ingredients:

• 2 tbsp dried oregano
• 2 tbsp dried thyme
• 2 tbsp dried marjoram
• 2 tbsp dried rosemary
• 2 tsp fennel seeds, toasted

Directions:

1. Mix the oregano, thyme, marjoram, rosemary, and fennel seeds in a bowl. Store the spices in an airtight container at room temperature for up to 7-9 months.

Nutrition Info:

• Info Per Serving: Calories: 32;Fat: 1.1g;Protein: 1.4g;Carbs: 6.0g.

Pepper & Cheese Stuffed Tomatoes

Servings:2
Cooking Time:35 Minutes

Ingredients:

• ½ lb mixed bell peppers, chopped
• 1 tbsp olive oil
• 4 tomatoes
• 2 garlic cloves, minced
• ½ cup diced onion
• 1 tbsp chopped oregano
• 1 tbsp chopped basil
• 1 cup shredded mozzarella
• 1 tbsp grated Parmesan cheese
• Salt and black pepper to taste

Directions:

1. Preheat oven to 370 F. Cut the tops of the tomatoes and scoop out the pulp. Chop the pulp and set aside. Arrange the tomatoes on a lined with parchment paper baking sheet.
2. Warm the olive oil in a pan over medium heat. Add in garlic, onion, basil, bell peppers, and oregano, and cook for 5 minutes. Sprinkle with salt and pepper. Remove from the heat and mix in tomato pulp and mozzarella cheese. Divide the mixture between the tomatoes and top with Parmesan cheese. Bake for 20 minutes or until the cheese melts. Serve.

Nutrition Info:

• Info Per Serving: Calories: 285;Fat: 10g;Protein: 24g;Carbs: 28g.

Mushroom & Parmesan Risotto

Servings:4
Cooking Time:25 Minutes

Ingredients:

• 1 ½ cups mixed mushrooms, sliced
• 3 tbsp olive oil
• 1 shallot, chopped
  1 cup Arborio rice

• 4 cups vegetable stock
• 2 tbsp dry white wine
• 1 cup grated Parmesan cheese
• 2 tbsp butter
• 2 tbsp fresh parsley, chopped

Directions:

1. Pour the vegetable stock into a small saucepan over low heat and bring to a simmer; then turn the heat off.
2. Warm the olive oil in a large saucepan over medium heat. Sauté the mushrooms and shallot for 6 minutes until tender. Stir in rice for 3 minutes until opaque. Pour in the wine and stir. Gradually add the hot stock to the rice mixture, about 1 ladleful at a time, stirring until the liquid is absorbed. Remove the saucepan from the heat, stir in butter and 3 tbsp of Parmesan cheese. Cover and leave to rest for 5 minutes. Scatter the remaining cheese and parsley over the risotto and serve in bowls.

Nutrition Info:

• Info Per Serving: Calories: 354;Fat: 29g;Protein: 11g;Carbs: 22g.

Octopus, Calamari & Watercress Salad

Servings:4
Cooking Time:50 Minutes

Ingredients:

• 2 tbsp olive oil
• 2 cups olives, sliced
• 1 octopus, tentacles separated
• 2 oz calamari rings
• 3 garlic cloves, minced
• 1 white onion, chopped
• ¾ cup chicken stock
• 2 cups watercress, sliced
• 1 cup parsley, chopped
• Salt and black pepper to taste
• 1 tbsp red wine vinegar

Directions:

1. Place octopus, stock, calamari rings, salt, and pepper in a pot over medium heat and bring to a simmer. Cook for 40 minutes. Strain seafood and let cool completely. Chop tentacles into pieces. Remove to a serv-

ing bowl along with the calamari rings. Stir in garlic, onion, watercress, olives, parsley, red wine vinegar, and olive oil and toss to coat.

Nutrition Info:

- Info Per Serving: Calories: 300;Fat: 11g;Protein: 9g;Carbs: 23g.

Feta & Cannellini Bean Soup

Servings:4
Cooking Time:30 Minutes

Ingredients:

- 2 tbsp olive oil
- 4 oz feta cheese, crumbled
- 1 cup collard greens, torn
- 2 cups canned cannellini beans
- 1 fennel bulb, chopped
- 1 carrot, chopped
- ½ cup spring onions, chopped
- ½ tsp dried rosemary
- ½ tsp dried basil
- 1 garlic clove, minced
- 4 cups vegetable broth
- 2 tbsp tomato paste
- Salt and black pepper to taste

Directions:

1. In a pot over medium heat, warm the olive oil. Add in fennel, garlic, carrot, and spring onions and sauté until tender, about 2-3 minutes. Stir in tomato paste, rosemary, and basil and cook for 2 more minutes. Pour in vegetable broth and cannellini beans. Bring to a boil, then lower the heat, and simmer for 15 minutes. Add in collard greens and cook for another 2-3 minutes until wilted. Adjust the seasoning with salt and pepper. Top with feta cheese and serve.

Nutrition Info:

- Info Per Serving: Calories: 519;Fat: 15g;Protein: 32g;Carbs: 65g.

Sweet Chickpea & Mushroom Stew

Servings:4
Cooking Time:20 Minutes

Ingredients:

- ½ tbsp button mushrooms, chopped
- 1 cup chickpeas, cooked
- 1 onion, peeled, chopped
- 1 lb string beans, trimmed
- 1 apple, cut into 1-inch cubes
- ½ cup raisins
- 2 carrots, chopped
- 2 garlic cloves, crushed
- 4 cherry tomatoes
- 2 tbsp fresh mint, chopped
- 1 tsp grated ginger
- ½ cup orange juice
- ½ tsp salt

Directions:

1. Place all ingredients in the instant pot. Pour enough water to cover. Cook on High Pressure for 8 minutes. Do a natural release for 10 minutes.

Nutrition Info:

- Info Per Serving: Calories: 350;Fat: 3.7g;Protein: 14g;Carbs: 71g.

Lemon And Spinach Orzo

Servings:2
Cooking Time: 10 Minutes

Ingredients:

- 1 cup dry orzo
- 1 bag baby spinach
- 1 cup halved grape tomatoes
- 2 tablespoons extra-virgin olive oil
- ¼ teaspoon salt
- Freshly ground black pepper
- ¾ cup crumbled feta cheese
- 1 lemon, juiced and zested

Directions:

1. Bring a medium pot of water to a boil. Stir in the orzo and cook uncovered for 8 minutes. Drain the water, then return the orzo to medium heat.

2. Add the spinach and tomatoes and cook until the spinach is wilted.

3. Sprinkle with the olive oil, salt, and pepper and mix well. Top with the feta cheese, lemon juice and zest, then toss one or two more times and serve.

Nutrition Info:

• Info Per Serving: Calories: 610;Fat: 27.0g;Protein: 21.0g;Carbs: 74.0g.

Cherry, Plum, Artichoke, And Cheese Board

Servings:4
Cooking Time: 0 Minutes

Ingredients:

• 2 cups rinsed cherries
• 2 cups rinsed and sliced plums
• 2 cups rinsed carrots, cut into sticks
• 1 cup canned low-sodium artichoke hearts, rinsed and drained
• 1 cup cubed feta cheese

Directions:

1. Arrange all the ingredients in separated portions on a clean board or a large tray, then serve with spoons, knife, and forks.

Nutrition Info:

• Info Per Serving: Calories: 417;Fat: 13.8g;Protein: 20.1g;Carbs: 56.2g.

Greens, Fennel, And Pear Soup With Cashews

Servings:4
Cooking Time: 15 Minutes

Ingredients:

• 2 tablespoons olive oil
• 1 fennel bulb, cut into ¼-inch-thick slices
• 2 leeks, white part only, sliced
• 2 pears, peeled, cored, and cut into ½-inch cubes
• 1 teaspoon sea salt
• ¼ teaspoon freshly ground black pepper
• ½ cup cashews
• 2 cups packed blanched spinach

• 3 cups low-sodium vegetable soup

Directions:

1. Heat the olive oil in a stockpot over high heat until shimmering.

2. Add the fennel and leeks, then sauté for 5 minutes or until tender.

3. Add the pears and sprinkle with salt and pepper, then sauté for another 3 minutes or until the pears are soft.

4. Add the cashews, spinach, and vegetable soup. Bring to a boil. Reduce the heat to low. Cover and simmer for 5 minutes.

5. Pour the soup in a food processor, then pulse until creamy and smooth.

6. Pour the soup back to the pot and heat over low heat until heated through.

7. Transfer the soup to a large serving bowl and serve immediately.

Nutrition Info:

• Info Per Serving: Calories: 266;Fat: 15.1g;Protein: 5.2g;Carbs: 32.9g.

Favorite Green Bean Stir-fry

Servings:4
Cooking Time:15 Minutes

Ingredients:

• 1 tbsp olive oil
• 1 tbsp butter
• 1 fennel bulb, sliced
• 1 red onion, sliced
• 4 cloves garlic, pressed
• 1 lb green beans, steamed
• ½ tsp dried oregano
• 2 tbsp balsamic vinegar
• Salt and black pepper to taste

Directions:

1. Heat the butter and olive oil a saucepan over medium heat. Add in the onion and garlic and sauté for 3 minutes. Stir in oregano, fennel, balsamic vinegar, salt, and pepper. Stir-fry for another 6-8 minutes and add in the green beans; cook for 2-3 minutes. Adjust the seasoning and serve.

Nutrition Info:

• Info Per Serving: Calories: 126;Fat: 6g;Protein: 3.3g;Carbs: 16.6g.

Traditional Panzanella Salad

Servings:2
Cooking Time:25 Minutes

Ingredients:

• 1 tbsp olive oil
• 4 French baguette slices, cubed
• 6 cherry tomatoes, halved
• 1 cucumber, cubed
• 1 sweet pepper, chopped
• 4 sweet onion thin slices
• ½ cup fresh basil leaves
• ¼ cup honey balsamic dressing

Directions:

1. Warm the oil in a pan over medium heat. Add the bread and salt and cook for 8-10 minutes, tossing frequently, or until nicely browned; let cool. Mix the cherry tomatoes, cucumber, pepper, onion, basil, and dressing and toss to coat in a large bowl. Top with bread cubes. Leave the salad to sit for about 20 minutes for the flavors to blend. Serve.

Nutrition Info:

• Info Per Serving: Calories: 525;Fat: 26g;Protein: 16g;Carbs: 61g.

Broccoli & Garlic Stir Fry

Servings:4
Cooking Time:15 Minutes

Ingredients:

• 1 red bell pepper, cut into chunks
• 3 tbsp olive oil
• 2 garlic cloves, minced
• ½ tsp red pepper flakes
• ½ lb broccoli florets
• Salt to taste
• 2 tsp lemon juice
• 1 tbsp anchovy paste

Directions:

1. Warm the olive oil in a skillet over medium heat. Add the broccoli, garlic, and red pepper flakes and stir briefly for 3-4 minutes until the florets turn bright green. Season with salt. Add 2 tbsp of water and let broccoli cook for another 2–3 minutes. Stir in the red bell pepper, lemon juice, and anchovy paste and cook for 1 more minute. Serve immediately.

Nutrition Info:

• Info Per Serving: Calories: 114;Fat: 11g;Protein: 3g;Carbs: 4g.

Simple Mushroom Barley Soup

Servings:6
Cooking Time: 20 To 23 Minutes

Ingredients:

• 2 tablespoons extra-virgin olive oil
• 1 cup chopped carrots
• 1 cup chopped onion
• 5½ cups chopped mushrooms
• 6 cups no-salt-added vegetable broth
• 1 cup uncooked pearled barley
• ¼ cup red wine
• 2 tablespoons tomato paste
• 4 sprigs fresh thyme or ½ teaspoon dried thyme
• 1 dried bay leaf
• 6 tablespoons grated Parmesan cheese

Directions:

1. In a large stockpot over medium heat, heat the oil. Add the onion and carrots and cook for 5 minutes, stirring frequently. Turn up the heat to medium-high and add the mushrooms. Cook for 3 minutes, stirring frequently.

2. Add the broth, barley, wine, tomato paste, thyme, and bay leaf. Stir, cover, and bring the soup to a boil. Once it's boiling, stir a few times, reduce the heat to medium-low, cover, and cook for another 12 to 15 minutes, until the barley is cooked through.

3. Remove the bay leaf and serve the soup in bowls with 1 tablespoon of cheese sprinkled on top of each.

Nutrition Info:

• Info Per Serving: Calories: 195;Fat: 4.0g;Protein 7.0g;Carbs: 34.0g.

Vegetable Mains And Meatless Recipes

Sweet Pepper Stew

Servings:2
Cooking Time: 50 Minutes

Ingredients:

- 2 tablespoons olive oil
- 2 sweet peppers, diced
- ½ large onion, minced
- 1 garlic clove, minced
- 1 tablespoon gluten-free Worcestershire sauce
- 1 teaspoon oregano
- 1 cup low-sodium tomato juice
- 1 cup low-sodium vegetable stock
- ¼ cup brown rice
- ¼ cup brown lentils
- Salt, to taste

Directions:

1. In a Dutch oven, heat the olive oil over medium-high heat.
2. Sauté the sweet peppers and onion for 10 minutes, stirring occasionally, or until the onion begins to turn golden and the peppers are wilted.
3. Stir in the garlic, Worcestershire sauce, and oregano and cook for 30 seconds more. Add the tomato juice, vegetable stock, rice, and lentils to the Dutch oven and stir to mix well.
4. Bring the mixture to a boil and then reduce the heat to medium-low. Let it simmer covered for about 45 minutes, or until the rice is cooked through and the lentils are tender.
5. Sprinkle with salt and serve warm.

Nutrition Info:

- Info Per Serving: Calories: 378;Fat: 15.6g;Protein: 11.4g;Carbs: 52.8g.

Garlicky Zucchini Cubes With Mint

Servings:4
Cooking Time: 10 Minutes

Ingredients:

- 3 large green zucchinis, cut into ½-inch cubes
- 3 tablespoons extra-virgin olive oil
- 1 large onion, chopped
- 3 cloves garlic, minced
- 1 teaspoon salt
- 1 teaspoon dried mint

Directions:

1. Heat the olive oil in a large skillet over medium heat.
2. Add the onion and garlic and sauté for 3 minutes, stirring constantly, or until softened.
3. Stir in the zucchini cubes and salt and cook for 5 minutes, or until the zucchini is browned and tender.
4. Add the mint to the skillet and toss to combine, then continue cooking for 2 minutes.
5. Serve warm.

Nutrition Info:

- Info Per Serving: Calories: 146;Fat: 10.6g;Protein: 4.2g;Carbs: 11.8g.

Tasty Lentil Burgers

Servings:4
Cooking Time:25 Minutes

Ingredients:

- 1 cup cremini mushrooms, finely chopped
- 1 cup cooked green lentils
- ½ cup Greek yogurt
- ½ lemon, zested and juiced
- ½ tsp garlic powder
- ½ tsp dried oregano
- 1 tbsp fresh cilantro, chopped
- Salt to taste
- 3 tbsp extra-virgin olive oil
- ¼ tsp tbsp white miso
- ¼ tsp smoked paprika
- ¼ cup flour

Directions:

1. Pour ½ cup of lentils in your blender and puree partially until somewhat smooth, but with many whole lentils still remaining. In a small bowl, mix the yogurt, lemon zest and juice, garlic powder, oregano, cilantro, and salt. Season and set aside. In a medium bowl, mix the mushrooms, 2 tablespoons of olive oil, miso, and paprika. Stir in all the lentils. Add in flour and stir until the mixture everything is well incorporated. Shape the mixture into patties about ¾-inch thick. Warm the remaining olive oil in a skillet over medium heat. Fry the patties until browned and crisp, about 3 minutes. Turn and fry on the second side. Serve with the reserved yogurt mixture.

Nutrition Info:

- Info Per Serving: Calories: 215;Fat: 13g;Protein: 10g;Carbs: 19g.

Stir-fried Kale With Mushrooms

Servings:4
Cooking Time:10 Minutes

Ingredients:

- 1 cup cremini mushrooms, sliced
- 4 tbsp olive oil
- 1 small red onion, chopped
- 2 cloves garlic, thinly sliced
- 1 ½ lb curly kale
- 2 tomatoes, chopped
- 1 tsp dried oregano
- 1 tsp dried basil
- ½ tsp dried rosemary
- ½ tsp dried thyme
- Salt and black pepper to taste

Directions:

1. Warm the olive oil in a saucepan over medium heat. Sauté the onion and garlic for about 3 minutes or until they are softened. Add in the mushrooms, kale, and tomatoes, stirring to promote even cooking. Turn the heat to a simmer, add in the spices and cook for 5-6 minutes until the kale wilt.

Nutrition Info:

- Info Per Serving: Calories: 221;Fat: 16g;Protein: 9g;Carbs: 19g.

Chargrilled Vegetable Kebabs

Servings:4
Cooking Time:26 Minutes

Ingredients:

- 2 red bell peppers, cut into squares
- 2 zucchinis, sliced into half-moons
- 6 portobello mushroom caps, quartered
- ¼ cup olive oil
- 1 tsp Dijon mustard
- 1 tsp fresh rosemary, chopped
- 1 garlic clove, minced
- Salt and black pepper to taste
- 2 red onions, cut into wedges

Directions:

1. Preheat your grill to High. Mix the olive oil, mustard, rosemary, garlic, salt, and pepper in a bowl. Reserve half of the oil mixture for serving. Thread the vegetables in alternating order onto metal skewers and brush them with the remaining oil mixture. Grill them for about 15 minutes until browned, turning occasionally. Transfer the kebabs to a serving platter and remove the skewers. Drizzle with reserved oil mixture and serve.

Nutrition Info:

• Info Per Serving: Calories: 96;Fat: 9.2g;Protein: 1.1g;Carbs: 3.6g.

Stuffed Portobello Mushroom With Tomatoes

Servings:4
Cooking Time: 15 Minutes

Ingredients:

• 4 large portobello mushroom caps
• 3 tablespoons extra-virgin olive oil
• Salt and freshly ground black pepper, to taste
• 4 sun-dried tomatoes
• 1 cup shredded mozzarella cheese, divided
• ½ to ¾ cup low-sodium tomato sauce

Directions:

1. Preheat the broiler on high.
2. Arrange the mushroom caps on a baking sheet and drizzle with olive oil. Sprinkle with salt and pepper.
3. Broil for 1o minutes, flipping the mushroom caps halfway through, until browned on the top.
4. Remove from the broil. Spoon 1 tomato, 2 tablespoons of cheese, and 2 to 3 tablespoons of sauce onto each mushroom cap.
5. Return the mushroom caps to the broiler and continue broiling for 2 to 3 minutes.
6. Cool for 5 minutes before serving.

Nutrition Info:

• Info Per Serving: Calories: 217;Fat: 15.8g;Protein: 11.2g;Carbs: 11.7g.

Sweet Potato Chickpea Buddha Bowl

Servings:2
Cooking Time: 10 To 15 Minutes

Ingredients:

• Sauce:
• 1 tablespoon tahini
• 2 tablespoons plain Greek yogurt
• 2 tablespoons hemp seeds
• 1 garlic clove, minced
• Pinch salt
• Freshly ground black pepper, to taste
• Bowl:

• 1 small sweet potato, peeled and finely diced
• 1 teaspoon extra-virgin olive oil
• 1 cup from 1 can low-sodium chickpeas, drained and rinsed
• 2 cups baby kale

Directions:

1. Make the Sauce
2. Whisk together the tahini and yogurt in a small bowl.
3. Stir in the hemp seeds and minced garlic. Season with salt pepper. Add 2 to 3 tablespoons water to create a creamy yet pourable consistency and set aside.
4. Make the Bowl
5. Preheat the oven to 425ºF. Line a baking sheet with parchment paper.
6. Place the sweet potato on the prepared baking sheet and drizzle with the olive oil. Toss well
7. Roast in the preheated oven for 10 to 15 minutes, stirring once during cooking, or until fork-tender and browned.
8. In each of 2 bowls, place ½ cup of chickpeas, 1 cup of baby kale, and half of the cooked sweet potato. Serve drizzled with half of the prepared sauce.

Nutrition Info:

• Info Per Serving: Calories: 323;Fat: 14.1g;Protein: 17.0g;Carbs: 36.0g.

Simple Broccoli With Yogurt Sauce

Servings:4
Cooking Time:25 Minutes

Ingredients:

• 2 tbsp olive oil
• 1 head broccoli, cut into florets
• 2 garlic cloves, minced
• ½ cup Greek yogurt
• Salt and black pepper to taste
• 2 tsp fresh dill, chopped

Directions:

1. Warm olive oil in a pan over medium heat and sauté broccoli, salt, and pepper for 12 minutes. Mix Greek yogurt, dill, and garlic in a small bowl. Drizzle the broccoli with the sauce.

Nutrition Info:

• Info Per Serving: Calories: 104;Fat: 7.7g;Protein: 4.5g;Carbs: 6g.

Zucchini And Artichokes Bowl With Farro

Servings:4
Cooking Time: 10 Minutes

Ingredients:

• ⅓ cup extra-virgin olive oil
• ⅓ cup chopped red onions
• ½ cup chopped red bell pepper
• 2 garlic cloves, minced
• 1 cup zucchini, cut into ½-inch-thick slices
• ½ cup coarsely chopped artichokes
• ½ cup canned chickpeas, drained and rinsed
• 3 cups cooked farro
• Salt and freshly ground black pepper, to taste
• ½ cup crumbled feta cheese, for serving (optional)
• ¼ cup sliced olives, for serving (optional)
• 2 tablespoons fresh basil, chiffonade, for serving (optional)
• 3 tablespoons balsamic vinegar, for serving (optional)

Directions:

1. Heat the olive oil in a large skillet over medium heat until it shimmers.
2. Add the onions, bell pepper, and garlic and sauté for 5 minutes, stirring occasionally, until softened.
3. Stir in the zucchini slices, artichokes, and chickpeas and sauté for about 5 minutes until slightly tender.
4. Add the cooked farro and toss to combine until heated through. Sprinkle the salt and pepper to season.
5. Divide the mixture into bowls. Top each bowl evenly with feta cheese, olive slices, and basil and sprinkle with the balsamic vinegar, if desired.

Nutrition Info:

• Info Per Serving: Calories: 366;Fat: 19.9g;Protein: 9.3g;Carbs: 50.7g.

Authentic Mushroom Gratin

Servings:4
Cooking Time:25 Minutes

Ingredients:

• 2 lb Button mushrooms, cleaned
• 2 tbsp olive oil
• 2 tomatoes, sliced
• 2 tomato paste
• ½ cup Parmesan cheese, grated
• ½ cup dry white wine
• ¼ tsp sweet paprika
• ½ tsp dried basil
• ½ tsp dried thyme
• Salt and black pepper to taste

Directions:

1. Preheat oven to 360 F. Combine tomatoes, tomato paste, wine, oil, mushrooms, paprika, black pepper, salt, basil, and thyme in a baking dish. Bake for 15 minutes. Top with Parmesan and continue baking for 5 minutes until the cheese melts.

Nutrition Info:

• Info Per Serving: Calories: 162;Fat: 8.6g;Protein: 9g;Carbs: 12.3g.

Roasted Caramelized Root Vegetables

Servings:6
Cooking Time:40 Minutes

Ingredients:

• 1 sweet potato, peeled and cut into chunks
• 3 tbsp olive oil
• 2 carrots, peeled
• 2 beets, peeled
• 1 turnip, peeled
• 1 tsp cumin
• 1 tsp sweet paprika
• Salt and black pepper to taste
• 1 lemon, juiced
• 2 tbsp parsley, chopped

Directions:

1. Preheat oven to 400 F. Cut the vegetables into chunks and toss them with olive oil and seasonings in

a sheet pan. Drizzle with lemon juice and roast them for 35-40 minutes until vegetables are tender and golden. Serve topped with parsley.

Nutrition Info:

• Info Per Serving: Calories: 80;Fat: 4.8g;Protein: 1.5g;Carbs: 8.9g.

Tahini & Feta Butternut Squash

Servings:6
Cooking Time:50 Minutes

Ingredients:

• 3 lb butternut squash, peeled, halved lengthwise, and seeded
• 3 tbsp olive oil
• Salt and black pepper to taste
• 2 tbsp fresh thyme, chopped
• 1 tbsp tahini
• 1 ½ tsp lemon juice
• 1 tsp honey
• 1 oz feta cheese, crumbled
• ¼ cup pistachios, chopped

Directions:

1. Preheat oven to 425 F. Slice the squash halves crosswise into ½-inch-thick pieces. Toss them with 2 tablespoons of olive oil, salt, and pepper and arrange them on a greased baking sheet in an even layer. Roast for 45-50 minutes or until golden and tender. Transfer squash to a serving platter. Whisk tahini, lemon juice, honey, remaining oil, and salt together in a bowl. Drizzle squash with tahini dressing and sprinkle with feta, pistachios, and thyme. Serve and enjoy!

Nutrition Info:

• Info Per Serving: Calories: 212;Fat: 12g;Protein: 4.1g;Carbs: 27g.

Baked Potato With Veggie Mix

Servings:4
Cooking Time:45 Minutes

Ingredients:

• 4 tbsp olive oil
• 1 lb potatoes, peeled and diced
• 2 red bell peppers, halved

• 1 lb mushrooms, sliced
• 2 tomatoes, diced
• 8 garlic cloves, peeled
• 1 eggplant, sliced
• 1 yellow onion, quartered
• ½ tsp dried oregano
• ¼ tsp caraway seeds
• Salt to taste

Directions:

1. Preheat the oven to 390 F. In a bowl, combine the bell peppers, mushrooms, tomatoes, eggplant, onion, garlic, salt, olive oil, oregano, and caraway seeds. Set aside. Arrange the potatoes on a baking dish and bake for 15 minutes. Top with the veggies mixture and bake for 15-20 minutes until tender.

Nutrition Info:

• Info Per Serving: Calories: 302;Fat: 15g;Protein: 8.5g;Carbs: 39g.

Balsamic Cherry Tomatoes

Servings:4
Cooking Time:10 Minutes

Ingredients:

• 2 tbsp olive oil
• 2 lb cherry tomatoes, halved
• 2 tbsp balsamic glaze
• Salt and black pepper to taste
• 1 garlic clove, minced
• 2 tbsp fresh basil, torn

Directions:

1. Warm the olive oil in a skillet over medium heat. Add the cherry tomatoes and cook for 1-2 minutes stirring occasionally. Stir in garlic, salt, and pepper and cook until fragrant, about 30 seconds. Drizzle with balsamic glaze and decorate with basil. Serve and enjoy!

Nutrition Info:

• Info Per Serving: Calories: 45;Fat: 2.5g;Protein: 1.1g;Carbs: 5.6g.

Eggplant And Zucchini Gratin

Servings:6
Cooking Time: 19 Minutes

Ingredients:

- 2 large zucchinis, finely chopped
- 1 large eggplant, finely chopped
- ¼ teaspoon kosher salt
- ¼ teaspoon freshly ground black pepper
- 3 tablespoons extra-virgin olive oil, divided
- ¾ cup unsweetened almond milk
- 1 tablespoon all-purpose flour
- ⅓ cup plus 2 tablespoons grated Parmesan cheese, divided
- 1 cup chopped tomato
- 1 cup diced fresh Mozzarella
- ¼ cup fresh basil leaves

Directions:

1. Preheat the oven to 425°F.
2. In a large bowl, toss together the zucchini, eggplant, salt and pepper.
3. In a large skillet over medium-high heat, heat 1 tablespoon of the oil. Add half of the veggie mixture to the skillet. Stir a few times, then cover and cook for about 4 minutes, stirring occasionally. Pour the cooked veggies into a baking dish. Place the skillet back on the heat, add 1 tablespoon of the oil and repeat with the remaining veggies. Add the veggies to the baking dish.
4. Meanwhile, heat the milk in the microwave for 1 minute. Set aside.
5. Place a medium saucepan over medium heat. Add the remaining 1 tablespoon of the oil and flour to the saucepan. Whisk together until well blended.
6. Slowly pour the warm milk into the saucepan, whisking the entire time. Continue to whisk frequently until the mixture thickens a bit. Add ⅓ cup of the Parmesan cheese and whisk until melted. Pour the cheese sauce over the vegetables in the baking dish and mix well.
7. Fold in the tomatoes and Mozzarella cheese. Roast in the oven for 10 minutes, or until the gratin is almost set and not runny.
8. Top with the fresh basil leaves and the remaining 2 tablespoons of the Parmesan cheese before serving.

Nutrition Info:

- Info Per Serving: Calories: 122;Fat: 5.0g;Protein: 10.0g;Carbs: 11.0g.

Stir-fried Eggplant

Servings:2
Cooking Time: 15 Minutes

Ingredients:

- 1 cup water, plus more as needed
- ½ cup chopped red onion
- 1 tablespoon finely chopped garlic
- 1 tablespoon dried Italian herb seasoning
- 1 teaspoon ground cumin
- 1 small eggplant, peeled and cut into ½-inch cubes
- 1 medium carrot, sliced
- 2 cups green beans, cut into 1-inch pieces
- 2 ribs celery, sliced
- 1 cup corn kernels
- 2 tablespoons almond butter
- 2 medium tomatoes, chopped

Directions:

1. Heat 1 tablespoon of water in a large soup pot over medium-high heat until it sputters.
2. Cook the onion for 2 minutes, adding a little more water as needed.
3. Add the garlic, Italian seasoning, cumin, and eggplant and stir-fry for 2 to 3 minutes, adding a little more water as needed.
4. Add the carrot, green beans, celery, corn kernels, and ½ cup of water and stir well. Reduce the heat to medium, cover, and cook for 8 to 10 minutes, stirring occasionally, or until the vegetables are tender.
5. Meanwhile, in a bowl, stir together the almond butter and ½ cup of water.
6. Remove the vegetables from the heat and stir in the almond butter mixture and chopped tomatoes. Cool for a few minutes before serving.

Nutrition Info:

- Info Per Serving: Calories: 176;Fat: 5.5g;Protein: 5.8g;Carbs: 25.4g.

Mushroom & Cauliflower Roast

Servings:4
Cooking Time:35 Minutes

Ingredients:

- 2 tbsp olive oil
- 4 cups cauliflower florets
- 1 celery stalk, chopped
- 1 cup mushrooms, sliced
- 10 cherry tomatoes, halved
- 1 yellow onion, chopped
- 2 garlic cloves, minced
- 2 tbsp dill, chopped
- Salt and black pepper to taste

Directions:

1. Preheat the oven to 340 F. Line a baking sheet with parchment paper. Place in cauliflower florets, olive oil, mushrooms, celery, tomatoes, onion, garlic, salt, and pepper and mix to combine. Bake for 25 minutes. Serve topped with dill.

Nutrition Info:

- Info Per Serving: Calories: 380;Fat: 15g;Protein: 12g;Carbs: 17g.

Wilted Dandelion Greens With Sweet Onion

Servings:4
Cooking Time: 15 Minutes

Ingredients:

- 1 tablespoon extra-virgin olive oil
- 2 garlic cloves, minced
- 1 Vidalia onion, thinly sliced
- ½ cup low-sodium vegetable broth
- 2 bunches dandelion greens, roughly chopped
- Freshly ground black pepper, to taste

Directions:

1. Heat the olive oil in a large skillet over low heat.
2. Add the garlic and onion and cook for 2 to 3 minutes, stirring occasionally, or until the onion is translucent.
3. Fold in the vegetable broth and dandelion greens and cook for 5 to 7 minutes until wilted, stirring fre-

quently.
4. Sprinkle with the black pepper and serve on a plate while warm.

Nutrition Info:

- Info Per Serving: Calories: 81;Fat: 3.9g;Protein: 3.2g;Carbs: 10.8g.

Sautéed Cabbage With Parsley

Servings:4
Cooking Time: 12 To 14 Minutes

Ingredients:

- 1 small head green cabbage, cored and sliced thin
- 2 tablespoons extra-virgin olive oil, divided
- 1 onion, halved and sliced thin
- ¾ teaspoon salt, divided
- ¼ teaspoon black pepper
- ¼ cup chopped fresh parsley
- 1½ teaspoons lemon juice

Directions:

1. Place the cabbage in a large bowl with cold water. Let sit for 3 minutes. Drain well.
2. Heat 1 tablespoon of the oil in a skillet over medium-high heat until shimmering. Add the onion and ¼ teaspoon of the salt and cook for 5 to 7 minutes, or until softened and lightly browned. Transfer to a bowl.
3. Heat the remaining 1 tablespoon of the oil in now-empty skillet over medium-high heat until shimmering. Add the cabbage and sprinkle with the remaining ½ teaspoon of the salt and black pepper. Cover and cook for about 3 minutes, without stirring, or until cabbage is wilted and lightly browned on bottom.
4. Stir and continue to cook for about 4 minutes, uncovered, or until the cabbage is crisp-tender and lightly browned in places, stirring once halfway through cooking. Off heat, stir in the cooked onion, parsley and lemon juice.
5. Transfer to a plate and serve.

Nutrition Info:

- Info Per Serving: Calories: 117;Fat: 7.0g;Protein: 2.7g;Carbs: 13.4g.

Simple Honey-glazed Baby Carrots

Servings:2
Cooking Time: 6 Minutes

Ingredients:

- ⅔ cup water
- 1½ pounds baby carrots
- 4 tablespoons almond butter
- ½ cup honey
- 1 teaspoon dried thyme
- 1½ teaspoons dried dill
- Salt, to taste

Directions:

1. Pour the water into the Instant Pot and add a steamer basket. Place the baby carrots in the basket.
2. Secure the lid. Select the Manual mode and set the cooking time for 4 minutes at High Pressure.
3. Once cooking is complete, do a quick pressure release. Carefully open the lid.
4. Transfer the carrots to a plate and set aside.
5. Pour the water out of the Instant Pot and dry it.
6. Press the Sauté button on the Instant Pot and heat the almond butter.
7. Stir in the honey, thyme, and dill.
8. Return the carrots to the Instant Pot and stir until well coated. Sauté for another 1 minute.
9. Taste and season with salt as needed. Serve warm.

Nutrition Info:

- Info Per Serving: Calories: 575;Fat: 23.5g;Protein: 2.8g;Carbs: 90.6g.

Italian Hot Green Beans

Servings:4
Cooking Time:25 Minutes

Ingredients:

- 2 tbsp olive oil
- 1 red bell pepper, diced
- 1 ½ lb green beans
- 4 garlic cloves, minced
- ½ tsp mustard seeds
- ½ tsp fennel seeds
- 1 tsp dried dill weed
- 2 tomatoes, chopped
- 1 cup cream of celery soup
- 1 tsp Italian herb mix
- 1 tsp chili powder
- Salt and black pepper to taste

Directions:

1. Warm the olive oil in a saucepan over medium heat. Add and fry the bell pepper and green beans for about 5 minutes, stirring periodically to promote even cooking. Add in the garlic, mustard seeds, fennel seeds, and dill and continue sautéing for an additional 1 minute or until fragrant. Add in the pureed tomatoes, cream of celery soup, Italian herb mix, chili powder, salt, and black pepper. Continue to simmer, covered, for 10-12 minutes until the green beans are tender.

Nutrition Info:

- Info Per Serving: Calories: 160;Fat: 9g;Protein: 5g;-Carbs: 19g.

Roasted Vegetable Medley

Servings:2
Cooking Time:65 Minutes

Ingredients:

- 1 head garlic, cloves split apart, unpeeled
- 3 tbsp olive oil
- 2 carrots, cut into strips
- ¼ lb asparagus, chopped
- ½ lb Brussels sprouts, halved
- 2 cups broccoli florets
- 1 cup cherry tomatoes
- ½ fresh lemon, sliced
- Salt and black pepper to taste

Directions:

1. Preheat oven to 375 F. Drizzle the garlic cloves with some olive oil and lightly wrap them in a small piece of foil. Place the packet in the oven and roast for 30 minutes. Place all the vegetables and the lemon slices into a large mixing bowl. Drizzle with the remaining olive oil and season with salt and pepper. Increase the oven to 400 F. Pour the vegetables on a sheet pan in a single layer, leaving the packet of garlic cloves on the pan. Roast for 20 minutes, shaking occasionally until tender. Remove the pan from the oven. Let the garlic cloves sit until cool enough to handle, then remove the

skins. Top the vegetables with roasted garlic and serve.

Nutrition Info:

• Info Per Serving: Calories: 256;Fat: 15g;Protein: 7g;Carbs: 31g.

Cauliflower Hash With Carrots

Servings:4
Cooking Time: 10 Minutes

Ingredients:

• 3 tablespoons extra-virgin olive oil
• 1 large onion, chopped
• 1 tablespoon minced garlic
• 2 cups diced carrots
• 4 cups cauliflower florets
• ½ teaspoon ground cumin
• 1 teaspoon salt

Directions:

1. In a large skillet, heat the olive oil over medium heat.
2. Add the onion and garlic and sauté for 1 minute. Stir in the carrots and stir-fry for 3 minutes.
3. Add the cauliflower florets, cumin, and salt and toss to combine.
4. Cover and cook for 3 minutes until lightly browned. Stir well and cook, uncovered, for 3 to 4 minutes, until softened.
5. Remove from the heat and serve warm.

Nutrition Info:

• Info Per Serving: Calories: 158;Fat: 10.8g;Protein: 3.1g;Carbs: 14.9g.

Cauliflower Rice Risotto With Mushrooms

Servings:4
Cooking Time: 10 Minutes

Ingredients:

• 1 teaspoon extra-virgin olive oil
• ½ cup chopped portobello mushrooms
• 4 cups cauliflower rice
• ½ cup half-and-half
• ¼ cup low-sodium vegetable broth

• 1 cup shredded Parmesan cheese

Directions:

1. In a medium skillet, heat the olive oil over medium-low heat until shimmering.
2. Add the mushrooms and stir-fry for 3 minutes.
3. Stir in the cauliflower rice, half-and-half, and vegetable broth. Cover and bring to a boil over high heat for 5 minutes, stirring occasionally.
4. Add the Parmesan cheese and stir to combine. Continue cooking for an additional 3 minutes until the cheese is melted.
5. Divide the mixture into four bowls and serve warm.

Nutrition Info:

• Info Per Serving: Calories: 167;Fat: 10.7g;Protein: 12.1g;Carbs: 8.1g.

Sautéed Green Beans With Tomatoes

Servings:4
Cooking Time: 20 Minutes

Ingredients:

• ¼ cup extra-virgin olive oil
• 1 large onion, chopped
• 4 cloves garlic, finely chopped
• 1 pound green beans, fresh or frozen, cut into 2-inch pieces
• 1½ teaspoons salt, divided
• 1 can diced tomatoes
• ½ teaspoon freshly ground black pepper

Directions:

1. Heat the olive oil in a large skillet over medium heat.
2. Add the onion and garlic and sauté for 1 minute until fragrant.
3. Stir in the green beans and sauté for 3 minutes Sprinkle with ½ teaspoon of salt.
4. Add the tomatoes, remaining salt, and pepper and stir to mix well. Cook for an additional 12 minutes stirring occasionally, or until the green beans are crisp and tender.
5. Remove from the heat and serve warm.

Nutrition Info:

• Info Per Serving: Calories: 219;Fat: 13.9g;Protein

4.0g;Carbs: 17.7g.

Vegetable And Red Lentil Stew

Servings:6
Cooking Time: 35 Minutes

Ingredients:

- 1 tablespoon extra-virgin olive oil
- 2 onions, peeled and finely diced
- 6½ cups water
- 2 zucchinis, finely diced
- 4 celery stalks, finely diced
- 3 cups red lentils
- 1 teaspoon dried oregano
- 1 teaspoon salt, plus more as needed

Directions:

1. Heat the olive oil in a large pot over medium heat.
2. Add the onions and sauté for about 5 minutes, stirring constantly, or until the onions are softened.
3. Stir in the water, zucchini, celery, lentils, oregano, and salt and bring the mixture to a boil.
4. Reduce the heat to low and let simmer covered for 30 minutes, stirring occasionally, or until the lentils are tender.
5. Taste and adjust the seasoning as needed.

Nutrition Info:

- Info Per Serving: Calories: 387;Fat: 4.4g;Protein: 24.0g;Carbs: 63.7g.

Zoodles With Beet Pesto

Servings:2
Cooking Time: 50 Minutes

Ingredients:

- 1 medium red beet, peeled, chopped
- ½ cup walnut pieces
- ½ cup crumbled goat cheese
- 3 garlic cloves
- 2 tablespoons freshly squeezed lemon juice
- 2 tablespoons plus 2 teaspoons extra-virgin olive oil, divided
- ¼ teaspoon salt
- 4 small zucchinis, spiralized

Directions:

1. Preheat the oven to 375ºF.
2. Wrap the chopped beet in a piece of aluminum foil and seal well.
3. Roast in the preheated oven for 30 to 40 minutes until tender.
4. Meanwhile, heat a skillet over medium-high heat until hot. Add the walnuts and toast for 5 to 7 minutes, or until fragrant and lightly browned.
5. Remove the cooked beets from the oven and place in a food processor. Add the toasted walnuts, goat cheese, garlic, lemon juice, 2 tablespoons of olive oil, and salt. Pulse until smoothly blended. Set aside.
6. Heat the remaining 2 teaspoons of olive oil in a large skillet over medium heat. Add the zucchini and toss to coat in the oil. Cook for 2 to 3 minutes, stirring gently, or until the zucchini is softened.
7. Transfer the zucchini to a serving plate and toss with the beet pesto, then serve.

Nutrition Info:

- Info Per Serving: Calories: 423;Fat: 38.8g;Protein: 8.0g;Carbs: 17.1g.

Spicy Potato Wedges

Servings:4
Cooking Time:30 Minutes

Ingredients:

- 1 ½ lb potatoes, peeled and cut into wedges
- 3 tbsp olive oil
- 1 tbsp minced fresh rosemary
- 2 tsp chili powder
- 3 garlic cloves, minced
- Salt and black pepper to taste

Directions:

1. Preheat the oven to 370 F. Toss the wedges with olive oil, garlic, salt, and pepper. Spread out in a roasting sheet. Roast for 15-20 minutes until browned and crisp at the edges. Remove and sprinkle with chili powder and rosemary.

Nutrition Info:

- Info Per Serving: Calories: 152;Fat: 7g;Protein: 2.5g;Carbs: 21g.

Lentil And Tomato Collard Wraps

Servings:4
Cooking Time: 0 Minutes

Ingredients:

- 2 cups cooked lentils
- 5 Roma tomatoes, diced
- ½ cup crumbled feta cheese
- 10 large fresh basil leaves, thinly sliced
- ¼ cup extra-virgin olive oil
- 1 tablespoon balsamic vinegar
- 2 garlic cloves, minced
- ½ teaspoon raw honey
- ½ teaspoon salt
- ¼ teaspoon freshly ground black pepper
- 4 large collard leaves, stems removed

Directions:

1. Combine the lentils, tomatoes, cheese, basil leaves, olive oil, vinegar, garlic, honey, salt, and black pepper in a large bowl and stir until well blended.
2. Lay the collard leaves on a flat work surface. Spoon the equal-sized amounts of the lentil mixture onto the edges of the leaves. Roll them up and slice in half to serve.

Nutrition Info:

- Info Per Serving: Calories: 318;Fat: 17.6g;Protein: 13.2g;Carbs: 27.5g.

Celery And Mustard Greens

Servings:4
Cooking Time: 15 Minutes

Ingredients:

- ½ cup low-sodium vegetable broth
- 1 celery stalk, roughly chopped
- ½ sweet onion, chopped
- ½ large red bell pepper, thinly sliced
- 2 garlic cloves, minced
- 1 bunch mustard greens, roughly chopped

Directions:

1. Pour the vegetable broth into a large cast iron pan and bring it to a simmer over medium heat.
2. Stir in the celery, onion, bell pepper, and garlic. Cook uncovered for about 3 to 5 minutes, or until the onion is softened.
3. Add the mustard greens to the pan and stir well. Cover, reduce the heat to low, and cook for an additional 10 minutes, or until the liquid is evaporated and the greens are wilted.
4. Remove from the heat and serve warm.

Nutrition Info:

- Info Per Serving: Calories: 39;Fat: 0g;Protein: 3.1g;Carbs: 6.8g.

Beans , Grains, And Pastas Recipes

Basic Brown Rice Pilaf With Capers

Servings:4
Cooking Time:30 Minutes

Ingredients:

- 2 tbsp olive oil
- 1 cup brown rice
- 1 onion, chopped
- 1 celery stalk, chopped
- 2 garlic cloves, minced
- ½ cup capers, rinsed
- Salt and black pepper to taste
- 2 tbsp parsley, chopped

Directions:

1. Warm the olive oil in a skillet over medium heat. Sauté celery, garlic, and onion for 10 minutes. Stir in rice, capers, 2 cups of water, salt, and pepper and cook for 25 minutes. Serve topped with parsley.

Nutrition Info:

- Info Per Serving: Calories: 230;Fat: 8.9g;Protein: 7g;Carbs: 16g.

Carrot & Caper Chickpeas

Servings:4
Cooking Time:35 Minutes

Ingredients:

- 3 tbsp olive oil
- 3 tbsp capers, drained
- 1 lemon, juiced and zested
- 1 red onion, chopped
- 14 oz canned chickpeas
- 4 carrots, peeled and cubed
- 1 tbsp parsley, chopped
- Salt and black pepper to taste

Directions:

1. Warm the olive oil in a skillet over medium heat and cook onion, lemon zest, lemon juice, and capers

for 5 minutes. Stir in chickpeas, carrots, parsley, salt, and pepper and cook for another 20 minutes. Serve and enjoy!

Nutrition Info:

- Info Per Serving: Calories: 210;Fat: 5g;Protein: 4g;-Carbs: 7g.

Sun-dried Tomato & Basil Risotto

Servings:4
Cooking Time:35 Minutes

Ingredients:

- 10 oz sundried tomatoes in olive oil, drained and chopped
- 2 tbsp olive oil
- 2 cups chicken stock
- 1 onion, chopped
- 1 cup Arborio rice
- Salt and black pepper to taste
- 1 cup Pecorino cheese, grated
- ¼ cup basil leaves, chopped

Directions:

1. Warm the olive oil in a skillet over medium heat and cook onion and sundried tomatoes for 5 minutes. Stir in rice, chicken stock, salt, pepper, and basil and bring to a boil. Cook for 20 minutes. Mix in Pecorino cheese and serve.

Nutrition Info:

- Info Per Serving: Calories: 430;Fat: 9g;Protein: 8g;-Carbs: 57g.

Spicy Italian Bean Balls With Marinara

Servings:2
Cooking Time: 30 Minutes

Ingredients:

- Bean Balls:
- 1 tablespoon extra-virgin olive oil
- ½ yellow onion, minced
- 1 teaspoon fennel seeds
- 2 teaspoons dried oregano
- ½ teaspoon crushed red pepper flakes
- 1 teaspoon garlic powder
- 1 can white beans (cannellini or navy), drained and rinsed
- ½ cup whole-grain bread crumbs
- Sea salt and ground black pepper, to taste
- Marinara:
- 1 tablespoon extra-virgin olive oil
- 3 garlic cloves, minced
- Handful basil leaves
- 1 can chopped tomatoes with juice reserved
- Sea salt, to taste

Directions:

1. Make the Bean Balls
2. Preheat the oven to 350°F. Line a baking sheet with parchment paper.
3. Heat the olive oil in a nonstick skillet over medium heat until shimmering.
4. Add the onion and sauté for 5 minutes or until translucent.
5. Sprinkle with fennel seeds, oregano, red pepper flakes, and garlic powder, then cook for 1 minute or until aromatic.
6. Pour the sautéed mixture in a food processor and add the beans and bread crumbs. Sprinkle with salt and ground black pepper, then pulse to combine well and the mixture holds together.
7. Shape the mixture into balls with a 2-ounce cookie scoop, then arrange the balls on the baking sheet.
8. Bake in the preheated oven for 30 minutes or until lightly browned. Flip the balls halfway through the cooking time.
9. Make the Marinara
10. While baking the bean balls, heat the olive oil in a saucepan over medium-high heat until shimmering.
11. Add the garlic and basil and sauté for 2 minutes or until fragrant.
12. Fold in the tomatoes and juice. Bring to a boil. Reduce the heat to low. Put the lid on and simmer for 15 minutes. Sprinkle with salt.
13. Transfer the bean balls on a large plate and baste with marinara before serving.

Nutrition Info:

- Info Per Serving: Calories: 351;Fat: 16.4g;Protein: 11.5g;Carbs: 42.9g.

Tomato Bean & Sausage Casserole

Servings:4
Cooking Time:45 Minutes

Ingredients:

- 2 tbsp olive oil
- 1 lb Italian sausages
- 1 can cannellini beans
- 1 carrot, chopped
- 1 onion, chopped
- 2 garlic cloves, minced
- 1 tsp paprika
- 1 can tomatoes, diced
- 1 celery stalk, chopped
- Salt and black pepper to taste

Directions:

1. Preheat oven to 350 F. Warm olive oil in a pot over medium heat. Sauté onion, garlic, celery, and carrot for 3-4 minutes, stirring often until softened. Add in sausages and cook for another 3 minutes, turning occasionally. Stir in paprika for 30 seconds. Heat off. Mix in tomatoes, beans, salt, and pepper. Pour into a baking dish and bake for 30 minutes.

Nutrition Info:

- Info Per Serving: Calories: 862;Fat: 44g;Protein: 43g;Carbs: 76g.

Cranberry & Walnut Freekeh Pilaf

Servings:4
Cooking Time:30 Minutes

Ingredients:

- 2 tbsp olive oil
- 2 ½ cups freekeh, soaked
- 2 medium onions, diced
- ¼ tsp ground cinnamon
- ¼ tsp ground allspice
- ¼ tsp ground nutmeg
- 5 cups chicken stock
- ½ cup walnuts, chopped
- Salt and black pepper to taste
- ½ cup Greek yogurt
- 1 ½ tsp lemon juice
- ½ tsp garlic powder
- 1 tbsp dried cranberries

Directions:

1. Warm the olive oil in a large skillet over medium heat and sauté the onions and cook until fragrant. Add the freekeh, cinnamon, nutmeg, and allspice. Stir for 1 minute. Pour in the stock, cranberries, and walnuts and season with salt and pepper. Bring to a simmer. Cover and reduce the heat to low.

2. Simmer for 15 minutes until the freekeh is tender. Remove from the heat and leave to sit for 5 minutes. In a small bowl, mix the yogurt, lemon juice, and garlic powder. Add the yogurt mixture to the freekeh and serve immediately.

Nutrition Info:

- Info Per Serving: Calories: 650;Fat: 25g;Protein: 12g;Carbs: 91g.

Cranberry And Almond Quinoa

Servings:2
Cooking Time: 10 Minutes

Ingredients:

- 2 cups water
- 1 cup quinoa, rinsed
- ¼ cup salted sunflower seeds
- ½ cup slivered almonds
- 1 cup dried cranberries

Directions:

1. Combine water and quinoa in the Instant Pot.
2. Secure the lid. Select the Manual mode and set the cooking time for 10 minutes at High Pressure.
3. Once cooking is complete, do a quick pressure release. Carefully open the lid.
4. Add sunflower seeds, almonds, and dried cranberries and gently mix until well combined.
5. Serve hot.

Nutrition Info:

- Info Per Serving: Calories: 445;Fat: 14.8g;Protein: 15.1g;Carbs: 64.1g.

Creamy Shrimp With Tie Pasta

Servings:4
Cooking Time:25 Minutes

Ingredients:

- 1 lb shrimp, peeled and deveined
- 1 tbsp olive oil
- 2 tbsp unsalted butter
- Salt and black pepper to taste
- 6 garlic cloves, minced
- ½ cup dry white wine
- 1 ½ cups heavy cream
- ½ cup grated Asiago cheese
- 2 tbsp chopped fresh parsley
- 16 oz bow tie pasta
- Salt to taste

Directions:

1. In a pot of boiling salted water, cook the tie pasta for 8-10 minutes until al dente. Drain and set aside.

2. Heat the olive oil in a large skillet, season the shrimp with salt and black pepper, and cook in the oil on both sides until pink and opaque, 2 minutes. Set aside. Melt the butter in the skillet and sauté the garlic until fragrant. Stir in the white wine and cook until reduced by half, scraping the bottom of the pan to deglaze. Reduce the heat to low and stir in the heavy cream. Allow simmering for 1 minute and stir in the Asiago cheese to melt. Return the shrimp to the sauce and sprinkle the parsley on top. Adjust the taste with salt and black pepper, if needed. Top the pasta with sauce and serve.

Nutrition Info:

• Info Per Serving: Calories: 493;Fat: 32g;Protein: 34g;Carbs: 16g.

Authentic Fava Bean & Garbanzo Fül

Servings:6
Cooking Time:20 Minutes

Ingredients:

• 3 tbsp extra-virgin olive oil
• 1 can garbanzo beans
• 1 can fava beans
• ½ tsp lemon zest
• ½ tsp dried oregano
• ½ cup lemon juice
• 3 cloves garlic, minced
• Salt to taste

Directions:

1. Place the garbanzo beans, fava beans, and 3 cups of water in a pot over medium heat. Cook for 10 minutes. Drain the beans Reserving 1 cup of the liquid, and put them in a bowl. Mix the reserved liquid, lemon juice, lemon zest, oregano, minced garlic, and salt together and add to the beans in the bowl. With a potato masher, mash up about half the beans in the bowl. Stir the mixture to combine. Drizzle the olive oil over the top. Serve with pita bread if desired.

Nutrition Info:

• Info Per Serving: Calories: 199;Fat: 9g;Protein: 10g;Carbs: 25g.

Lentil And Mushroom Pasta

Servings:2
Cooking Time: 50 Minutes

Ingredients:

2 tablespoons olive oil
1 large yellow onion, finely diced
2 portobello mushrooms, trimmed and chopped finely
2 tablespoons tomato paste
3 garlic cloves, chopped
1 teaspoon oregano
2½ cups water

• 1 cup brown lentils
• 1 can diced tomatoes with basil (with juice if diced)
• 1 tablespoon balsamic vinegar
• 8 ounces pasta of choice, cooked
• Salt and black pepper, to taste
• Chopped basil, for garnish

Directions:

1. Place a large stockpot over medium heat. Add the oil. Once the oil is hot, add the onion and mushrooms. Cover and cook until both are soft, about 5 minutes. Add the tomato paste, garlic, and oregano and cook 2 minutes, stirring constantly.
2. Stir in the water and lentils. Bring to a boil, then reduce the heat to medium-low and cook for 5 minutes, covered.
3. Add the tomatoes (and juice if using diced) and vinegar. Replace the lid, reduce the heat to low and cook until the lentils are tender, about 30 minutes.
4. Remove the sauce from the heat and season with salt and pepper to taste. Garnish with the basil and serve over the cooked pasta.

Nutrition Info:

• Info Per Serving: Calories: 463;Fat: 15.9g;Protein: 12.5g;Carbs: 70.8g.

Pasta In Dilly Walnut Sauce

Servings:4
Cooking Time:10 Minutes

Ingredients:

• 3 tbsp extra-virgin olive oil
• 8 oz whole-wheat pasta
• ¼ cup walnuts, chopped
• 3 garlic cloves, finely minced
• ½ cup fresh dill, chopped
• ¼ cup grated Parmesan cheese

Directions:

1. Cook the whole-wheat pasta according to pack instructions, drain and let it cool. Place the olive oil, dill, garlic, Parmesan cheese, and walnuts in a food processor and blend for 15 seconds or until paste forms. Pour over the cooled pasta and toss to combine. Serve immediately.

Nutrition Info:

• Info Per Serving: Calories: 559;Fat: 17g;Protein: 21g;Carbs: 91g.

Home-style Beef Ragu Rigatoni

Servings:6
Cooking Time:2 Hours

Ingredients:

• 1 tbsp olive oil
• 1 ½ lb bone-in short ribs
• Salt and black pepper to taste
• 1 onion, finely chopped
• 3 garlic cloves, minced
• 1 tsp fresh thyme, minced
• ½ tsp ground cinnamon
• A pinch of ground cloves
• ½ cup dry red wine
• 1 can tomatoes, diced
• 1 lb rigatoni
• 2 tbsp fresh parsley, minced
• 2 tbsp Pecorino cheese, grated

Directions:

1. Season the ribs with salt and pepper. Heat oil in a large skillet and brown the ribs on all sides, 7-10 minutes; transfer to a plate. Remove all but 1 tsp fat from skillet, add onion, and stir-fry over medium heat for 5 minutes. Stir in garlic, thyme, cinnamon, and cloves and cook until fragrant, 40 seconds. Pour in the wine, scraping off any browned bits, and simmer until almost evaporated, 2 minutes. Stir in tomatoes and their juice.
2. Nestle ribs into the sauce along with any accumulated juices and bring to a simmer. Lower the heat, cover and let simmer, turning the ribs from time to time until the meat is very tender and falling off bones, 2 hours. Transfer the ribs to cutting board, let cool slightly, then shred it using 2 forks; discard excess fat and bones.
3. Skim excess fat from the surface of the sauce with a spoon. Stir shredded meat and any accumulated juices into the sauce and bring to a simmer over medium heat. Season to taste. Meanwhile, bring a large pot filled with salted water to a boil and cook pasta until al dente. Reserve ½ cup of the cooking water, drain pasta and return it to pot. Add sauce and parsley and toss to combine. Season to taste and adjust consistency with

reserved cooking water as needed. Serve with freshly grated Pecorino cheese.

Nutrition Info:

• Info Per Serving: Calories: 415;Fat: 11g;Protein: 12g;Carbs: 42g.

Lebanese Flavor Broken Thin Noodles

Servings:6
Cooking Time: 25 Minutes

Ingredients:

• 1 tablespoon extra-virgin olive oil
• 1 cup vermicelli, broken into 1- to 1½-inch pieces
• 3 cups shredded cabbage
• 1 cup brown rice
• 3 cups low-sodium vegetable soup
• ½ cup water
• 2 garlic cloves, mashed
• ¼ teaspoon sea salt
• ⅛ teaspoon crushed red pepper flakes
• ½ cup coarsely chopped cilantro
• Fresh lemon slices, for serving

Directions:

1. Heat the olive oil in a saucepan over medium-high heat until shimmering.
2. Add the vermicelli and sauté for 3 minutes or until toasted.
3. Add the cabbage and sauté for 4 minutes or until tender.
4. Pour in the brown rice, vegetable soup, and water. Add the garlic and sprinkle with salt and red pepper flakes.
5. Bring to a boil over high heat. Reduce the heat to medium low. Put the lid on and simmer for another 10 minutes.
6. Turn off the heat, then let sit for 5 minutes without opening the lid.
7. Pour them on a large serving platter and spread with cilantro. Squeeze the lemon slices over and serve warm.

Nutrition Info:

• Info Per Serving: Calories: 127;Fat: 3.1g;Protein 4.2g;Carbs: 22.9g.

Parsley Beef Fusilli

Servings:4
Cooking Time:30 Minutes

Ingredients:

- 1 cup grated Pecorino Romano cheese
- 1 lb thick-cut New York strip steaks, cut into 1-inch cubes
- 4 tbsp butter
- 16 oz fusilli pasta
- Salt and black pepper to taste
- 4 garlic cloves, minced
- 2 tbsp chopped fresh parsley

Directions:

1. In a pot of boiling water, cook the fusilli pasta for 8-10 minutes until al dente. Drain and set aside.
2. Melt the butter in a large skillet, season the steaks with salt, black pepper and cook in the butter until brown, and cooked through, 10 minutes. Stir in the garlic and cook until fragrant, 1 minute. Mix in the parsley and fusilli pasta; toss well and season with salt and black pepper. Dish the food, top with the Pecorino Romano cheese and serve immediately.

Nutrition Info:

- Info Per Serving: Calories: 422;Fat: 22g;Protein: 36g;Carbs: 17g.

Hot Zucchini Millet

Servings:4
Cooking Time:30 Minutes

Ingredients:

- 3 tbsp olive oil
- 2 tomatoes, chopped
- 2 zucchinis, chopped
- 1 cup millet
  2 spring onions, chopped
  ½ cup cilantro, chopped
  1 tsp chili paste
  ½ cup lemon juice
  Salt and black pepper to taste

Directions:

. Warm the olive oil in a skillet over medium heat

and sauté millet for 1-2 minutes. Pour in 2 cups of water, salt, and pepper and bring to a simmer. Cook for 15 minutes. Mix in spring onions, tomatoes, zucchini, chili paste, and lemon juice. Serve topped with cilantro.

Nutrition Info:

- Info Per Serving: Calories: 230;Fat: 11g;Protein: 3g;Carbs: 15g.

Cherry, Apricot, And Pecan Brown Rice Bowl

Servings:2
Cooking Time: 1 Hour 1 Minutes

Ingredients:

- 2 tablespoons olive oil
- 2 green onions, sliced
- ½ cup brown rice
- 1 cup low -sodium chicken stock
- 2 tablespoons dried cherries
- 4 dried apricots, chopped
- 2 tablespoons pecans, toasted and chopped
- Sea salt and freshly ground pepper, to taste

Directions:

1. Heat the olive oil in a medium saucepan over medium-high heat until shimmering.
2. Add the green onions and sauté for 1 minutes or until fragrant.
3. Add the rice. Stir to mix well, then pour in the chicken stock.
4. Bring to a boil. Reduce the heat to low. Cover and simmer for 50 minutes or until the brown rice is soft.
5. Add the cherries, apricots, and pecans, and simmer for 10 more minutes or until the fruits are tender.
6. Pour them in a large serving bowl. Fluff with a fork. Sprinkle with sea salt and freshly ground pepper. Serve immediately.

Nutrition Info:

- Info Per Serving: Calories: 451;Fat: 25.9g;Protein: 8.2g;Carbs: 50.4g.

Lentil And Vegetable Curry Stew

Servings:8
Cooking Time: 4 Hours 7 Minutes

Ingredients:

- 1 tablespoon coconut oil
- 1 yellow onion, diced
- ¼ cup yellow Thai curry paste
- 2 cups unsweetened coconut milk
- 2 cups dry red lentils, rinsed well and drained
- 3 cups bite-sized cauliflower florets
- 2 golden potatoes, cut into chunks
- 2 carrots, peeled and diced
- 8 cups low-sodium vegetable soup, divided
- 1 bunch kale, stems removed and roughly chopped
- Sea salt, to taste
- ½ cup fresh cilantro, chopped
- Pinch crushed red pepper flakes

Directions:

1. Heat the coconut oil in a nonstick skillet over medium-high heat until melted.
2. Add the onion and sauté for 5 minutes or until translucent.
3. Pour in the curry paste and sauté for another 2 minutes, then fold in the coconut milk and stir to combine well. Bring to a simmer and turn off the heat.
4. Put the lentils, cauliflower, potatoes, and carrot in the slow cooker. Pour in 6 cups of vegetable soup and the curry mixture. Stir to combine well.
5. Cover and cook on high for 4 hours or until the lentils and vegetables are soft. Stir periodically.
6. During the last 30 minutes, fold the kale in the slow cooker and pour in the remaining vegetable soup. Sprinkle with salt.
7. Pour the stew in a large serving bowl and spread the cilantro and red pepper flakes on top before serving hot.

Nutrition Info:

- Info Per Serving: Calories: 530;Fat: 19.2g;Protein: 20.3g;Carbs: 75.2g.

Spicy Bean Rolls

Servings:4
Cooking Time:25 Minutes

Ingredients:

- 1 tbsp olive oil
- 1 red onion, chopped
- 2 garlic cloves, minced
- 1 green bell pepper, sliced
- 2 cups canned cannellini beans
- 1 red chili pepper, chopped
- 1 tbsp cilantro, chopped
- 1 tsp cumin, ground
- Salt and black pepper to taste
- 4 whole-wheat tortillas
- 1 cup mozzarella, shredded

Directions:

1. Warm the olive oil in a skillet over medium heat and sauté onion for 3 minutes. Stir in garlic, bell pepper, cannellini beans, red chili pepper, cilantro, cumin, salt, and pepper and cook for 15 minutes. Spoon bean mixture on each tortilla and top with cheese. Roll up and serve right away.

Nutrition Info:

- Info Per Serving: Calories: 680;Fat: 15g;Protein: 38g;Carbs: 75g.

Jalapeño Veggie Rice Stew

Servings:4
Cooking Time:45 Minutes

Ingredients:

- 2 tbsp olive oil
- 1 cup rice
- 1 lb green beans, chopped
- 2 zucchinis, sliced
- 1 bell pepper, sliced
- 1 jalapeño pepper, chopped
- 1 carrot, chopped
- 2 spring onions, chopped
- 2 cloves garlic, minced
- 2 tomatoes, pureed
- 1 cup vegetable broth
- ½ tsp dried sage

- 1 tsp paprika
- Salt and black pepper to taste

Directions:

1. Cook the rice in a pot with 2 cups of water for about 20 minutes. Using a fork, fluff the rice and set aside. Heat the olive oil in a pot over medium heat. Add in the zucchinis, green beans, bell pepper, jalapeño pepper, carrot, spring onions, tomatoes, and garlic and stir-fry for 10 minutes or until the veggies are softened. Pour in vegetable broth, sage, paprika, salt, and black pepper. Cook covered for 7 minutes. Distribute the rice across bowls and top with the veggie mixture. Serve hot.

Nutrition Info:

- Info Per Serving: Calories: 153;Fat: 7.9g;Protein: 5.7g;Carbs: 19g.

Veggie & Egg Quinoa With Pancetta

Servings:4
Cooking Time:35 Minutes

Ingredients:

- 4 pancetta slices, cooked and crumbled
- 2 tbsp olive oil
- 1 small red onion, chopped
- 1 red bell pepper, chopped
- 1 sweet potato, grated
- 1 green bell pepper, chopped
- 2 garlic cloves, minced
- 1 cup mushrooms, sliced
- ½ cup quinoa
- 1 cup chicken stock
- 4 eggs, fried
- ¼ tsp red pepper flakes
- Salt and black pepper to taste

Directions:

1. Warm the olive oil in a skillet over medium heat and cook onion, garlic, bell peppers, sweet potato, and mushrooms for 5 minutes, stirring often. Stir in quinoa for another minute. Mix in stock, salt, and pepper for 5 minutes. Share into plates and serve topped with fried eggs, salt, pepper, red pepper flakes, and crumbled pancetta.

Nutrition Info:

- Info Per Serving: Calories: 310;Fat: 15g;Protein: 16g;Carbs: 26g.

Tomato Basil Pasta

Servings:2
Cooking Time: 2 Minutes

Ingredients:

- 2 cups dried campanelle or similar pasta
- 1¾ cups vegetable stock
- ½ teaspoon salt, plus more as needed
- 2 tomatoes, cut into large dices
- 1 or 2 pinches red pepper flakes
- ½ teaspoon garlic powder
- ½ teaspoon dried oregano
- 10 to 12 fresh sweet basil leaves
- Freshly ground black pepper, to taste

Directions:

1. In your Instant Pot, stir together the pasta, stock, and salt. Scatter the tomatoes on top (do not stir).
2. Secure the lid. Select the Manual mode and set the cooking time for 2 minutes at High Pressure.
3. Once cooking is complete, do a quick pressure release. Carefully open the lid.
4. Stir in the red pepper flakes, oregano, and garlic powder. If there's more than a few tablespoons of liquid in the bottom, select Sauté and cook for 2 to 3 minutes until it evaporates.
5. When ready to serve, chiffonade the basil and stir it in. Taste and season with more salt and pepper, as needed. Serve warm.

Nutrition Info:

- Info Per Serving: Calories: 415;Fat: 2.0g;Protein: 15.2g;Carbs: 84.2g.

Parmesan Beef Rotini With Asparagus

Servings:4
Cooking Time:40 Minutes

Ingredients:

- 1 lb asparagus, cut into 1-inch pieces
- 3 tbsp olive oil
- 16 oz rotini pasta
- 1 lb ground beef
- 2 large shallots, chopped
- 3 garlic cloves, minced
- Salt and black pepper to taste
- 1 cup grated Parmesan cheese

Directions:

1. In a pot of boiling water, cook the rotini pasta for 8-10 minutes until al dente. Drain and set aside.
2. Heat a large non-stick skillet over medium heat and add the beef. Cook while breaking the lumps that form until brown, 10 minutes. Use a slotted spoon to transfer the beef to a plate and discard the drippings. Heat olive oil in a skillet and sauté asparagus until tender, 7 minutes. Stir in shallots and garlic and cook for 2 minutes. Season with salt and pepper. Stir in the beef and rotini pasta and toss until well combined. Adjust the taste with salt and black pepper as desired. Dish the food between serving plates and garnish with Parmesan.

Nutrition Info:

- Info Per Serving: Calories: 513;Fat: 25g;Protein: 44g;Carbs: 21g.

Black Bean Chili With Mangoes

Servings:4
Cooking Time: 10 Minutes

Ingredients:

- 2 tablespoons coconut oil
- 1 onion, chopped
- 2 cans black beans, drained and rinsed
- 1 tablespoon chili powder
- 1 teaspoon sea salt
- ¼ teaspoon freshly ground black pepper
- 1 cup water
- 2 ripe mangoes, sliced thinly
- ¼ cup chopped fresh cilantro, divided
- ¼ cup sliced scallions, divided

Directions:

1. Heat the coconut oil in a pot over high heat until melted.
2. Put the onion in the pot and sauté for 5 minutes or until translucent.
3. Add the black beans to the pot. Sprinkle with chili powder, salt, and ground black pepper. Pour in the water. Stir to mix well.
4. Bring to a boil. Reduce the heat to low, then simmering for 5 minutes or until the beans are tender.
5. Turn off the heat and mix in the mangoes, then garnish with scallions and cilantro before serving.

Nutrition Info:

- Info Per Serving: Calories: 430;Fat: 9.1g;Protein: 20.2g;Carbs: 71.9g.

Instant Pot Pork With Rice

Servings:4
Cooking Time:35 Minutes

Ingredients:

- 3 tbsp olive oil
- 1 lb pork stew meat, cubed
- Salt and black pepper to taste
- 2 chicken broth
- 1 leek, sliced
- 1 onion, chopped
- 1 carrot, sliced
- 1 cup brown rice
- 2 garlic cloves, minced
- 2 tbsp cilantro, chopped

Directions:

1. Set your Instant Pot to Sauté and heat the olive oil. Place in pork and cook for 4-5 minutes, stirring often. Add in onion, leek, garlic, and carrot and sauté for 3 more minutes. Stir in brown rice for 1 minute and pour in chicken broth; return the pork. Lock the lid in place, select Manual, and cook for 20 minutes on High. When done, do a quick pressure release. Adjust the seasoning and serve topped with cilantro.

Nutrition Info:

- Info Per Serving: Calories: 310;Fat: 16g;Protein: 23g;Carbs: 18g.

Creamy Asparagus & Parmesan Linguine

Servings:2
Cooking Time:30 Minutes

Ingredients:

- 2 tsp olive oil
- 1 bunch of asparagus spears
- 1 yellow onion, thinly sliced
- ¼ cup white wine
- ¼ cup vegetable stock
- 2 cups heavy cream
- ¼ tsp garlic powder
- 8 oz linguine
- ¼ cup Parmesan cheese
- 1 lemon, juiced
- Salt and black pepper to taste
- 2 tbsp chives, chopped

Directions:

1. Bring to a boil salted water in a pot over high heat. Add the linguine and cook according to package directions. Drain and transfer to a bowl. Slice the asparagus into bite-sized pieces. Warm the olive oil in a skillet over medium heat. Add onion and cook 3 minutes until softened. Add asparagus and wine and cook until wine is mostly evaporated, then add the stock. Stir in cream and garlic powder and bring to a boil and simmer until the sauce is slightly thick, 2-3 minutes. Add the linguine and stir until everything is heated through. Remove from the heat and season with lemon juice, salt, and pepper. Top with parmesan cheese and chives and serve.

Nutrition Info:

- Info Per Serving: Calories: 503;Fat: 55g;Protein: 24g;Carbs: 41g.

Herb Bean Stew

Servings:4
Cooking Time:70 Minutes

Ingredients:

- 2 tbsp olive oil
- 3 tomatoes, cubed
- 1 yellow onion, chopped
- 1 celery stalk, chopped
- 2 tbsp parsley, chopped
- 2 garlic cloves, minced
- 1 cup lima beans, soaked
- 1 tsp paprika
- 1 tsp dried oregano
- ½ tsp dried thyme
- Salt and black pepper to taste

Directions:

1. Cover the lima beans with water in a pot and place over medium heat. Bring to a boil and cook for 30 minutes. Drain and set aside. Warm olive oil in the pot over medium heat and cook onion and garlic for 3 minutes. Stir in tomatoes, celery, oregano, thyme, and paprika and cook for 5 minutes. Pour in 3 cups of water and return the lima beans; season with salt and pepper. Simmer for 30 minutes. Top with parsley.

Nutrition Info:

- Info Per Serving: Calories: 310;Fat: 16g;Protein: 16g;Carbs: 30g.

Mint Brown Rice

Servings:2
Cooking Time: 22 Minutes

Ingredients:

- 2 cloves garlic, minced
- ¼ cup chopped fresh mint, plus more for garnish
- 1 tablespoon chopped dried chives
- 1 cup short- or long-grain brown rice
- 1½ cups water or low-sodium vegetable broth
- ½ to 1 teaspoon sea salt

Directions:

1. Place the garlic, mint, chives, rice, and water in the Instant Pot. Stir to combine.
2. Secure the lid. Select the Manual mode and set the cooking time for 22 minutes at High Pressure.
3. Once cooking is complete, do a natural pressure release for 10 minutes, then release any remaining pressure. Carefully open the lid.
4. Add salt to taste. Serve garnished with more mint.

Nutrition Info:

- Info Per Serving: Calories: 514;Fat: 6.6g;Protein: 20.7g;Carbs: 80.4g.

Mediterranean Brown Rice

Servings:4
Cooking Time:20 Minutes

Ingredients:

- 1 lb asparagus, steamed and chopped
- 2 tbsp olive oil
- 3 tbsp balsamic vinegar
- 1 cup brown rice
- 2 tsp mustard
- Salt and black pepper to taste
- 5 oz baby spinach
- ½ cup parsley, chopped
- 1 tbsp tarragon, chopped

Directions:

1. Bring to a boil a pot of salted water over medium heat. Add in brown rice and cook for 7-9 minutes until al dente. Drain and place in a bowl. Add the asparagus to the same pot and blanch them for 4-5 minutes. Remove them to the rice bowl. Mix in spinach, olive oil, balsamic vinegar, mustard, salt, pepper, parsley, and tarragon. Serve.

Nutrition Info:

- Info Per Serving: Calories: 330;Fat: 12g;Protein: 11g;Carbs: 17g.

Lemon Couscous With Broccoli

Servings:4
Cooking Time:20 Minutes

Ingredients:

- 2 tsp olive oil
- Salt and black pepper to taste
- 1 small red onion, sliced
- 1 lemon, zested
- 1 head broccoli, cut into florets
- 1 cup couscous

Directions:

1. Heat a pot filled with salted water over medium heat; bring to a boil. Add in the broccoli and cook for 4-6 minutes until tender. Remove to a boil with a slotted spoon. In another bowl, place the couscous and cover with boiling broccoli water. Cover and let sit for 3-4 minutes until the water is absorbrd. Fluff the couscous with a fork and season with lemon zest, salt. and pepper. Stir in broccoli and top with red onion to serve.

Nutrition Info:

- Info Per Serving: Calories: 620;Fat: 45g;Protein: 11g;Carbs: 51g.

Classic Garidomakaronada (shrimp & Pasta)

Servings:4
Cooking Time:45 Minutes

Ingredients:

- 2 tbsp olive oil
- 16 medium shrimp, shelled and deveined
- Salt and black pepper to taste
- 1 onion, finely chopped
- 3 garlic cloves, minced
- 4 tomatoes, puréed
- ½ tsp sugar
- 1 tbsp tomato paste
- 1 tbsp ouzo
- 1 lb whole-wheat spaghetti
- ½ tsp crushed red pepper
- ¼ tsp dried Greek oregano
- 2 tbsp chopped fresh parsley

Directions:

1. Bring a large pot of salted water to a boil, add the spaghetti, and cook for 7-9 minutes until al dente. Drain the pasta and set aside. Warm the olive oil in a large skillet over medium heat. Sauté the shrimp for 2 minutes, flipping once or until pink; set aside. Add the onion and garlic to the skillet and cook for 3-5 minutes or until tender.

2. Add tomatoes, sugar, oregano, and tomato paste. Bring the sauce to a boil. Reduce the heat and simmer for 15–20 minutes or until thickened. Stir in ouzo and season with salt and black pepper. Add the pasta along with crushed red pepper and cooked shrimp. Remove from heat and toss to coat the pasta. Sprinkle with parsley and serve immediately.

Nutrition Info:

- Info Per Serving: Calories: 319;Fat: 9g;Protein 10g;Carbs: 51g.

Fruits, Desserts And Snacks Recipes

Pizza A La Portuguesa

Servings:4
Cooking Time:35 Minutes

Ingredients:

- For the crust
- 2 tbsp olive oil
- 2 cups flour
- 1 cup lukewarm water
- 1 pinch of sugar
- 1 tsp active dry yeast
- ¾ tsp salt
- For the topping
- 2 tbsp pizza sauce
- 2 red onions, thinly sliced
- 1 tsp dry oregano
- 2 cups shredded mozzarella
- 2 boiled eggs thinly sliced
- 12 green olives

Directions:

1. Sift the flour and salt in a bowl and stir in yeast. Mix lukewarm water, olive oil, and sugar in another bowl. Add the wet mixture to the dry mixture and whisk until you obtain a soft dough. Place the dough on a floured work surface and knead it thoroughly for 4-5 minutes until elastic. Transfer the dough to a greased bowl. Cover with cling film and leave to rise for 50-60 minutes in a warm place until doubled in size. Roll out the dough to a thickness of around 12 inches. Place on a pizza pan covered with parchment paper
2. Preheat the oven to 450 F. Spread the pizza sauce on the crust. Sprinkle with oregano, then mozzarella cheese, then the onions, and finally the olives. Bake in the oven for 10 minutes. Top with eggs and serve sliced into wedges..

Nutrition Info:

- Info Per Serving: Calories: 317;Fat: 20g;Protein: 28g;Carbs: 1g.

Spiced Nut Mix

Servings:6
Cooking Time:20 Minutes

Ingredients:

- 1 tbsp olive oil
- 2 cups raw mixed nuts
- 1 tsp ground cumin
- ½ tsp garlic powder
- ½ tsp kosher salt
- ⅛ tsp chili powder
- ⅛ tsp ground coriander

Directions:

1. Place the nuts in a skillet over medium heat and toast for 3 minutes, shaking the pan continuously. Remove to a bowl, season with salt, and reserve. Warm olive oil in the same skillet. Add in cumin, garlic powder, chili powder, and ground coriander and cook for about 20-30 seconds. Mix in nuts and cook for another 4 minutes. Serve chilled.

Nutrition Info:

- Info Per Serving: Calories: 315;Fat: 29.2g;Protein: 8g;Carbs: 11g.

Eggplant & Bell Pepper Spread

Servings:4
Cooking Time:55 Minutes

Ingredients:

- ¼ cup olive oil
- 1 cup light mayonnaise
- 2 eggplants, sliced
- Salt and black pepper to taste
- 4 garlic cloves, minced
- 1 tbsp chives, chopped

Directions:

1. Preheat the oven to 360 F. Arrange bell peppers and eggplants on a baking pan. Sprinkle with salt, peppe

and garlic and drizzle with some olive oil. Bake for 45 minutes. Transfer to a food processor and pulse until smooth a few times while gradually adding the remaining olive oil. Remove to a bowl and mix in mayonnaise. Top with chives and serve.

Nutrition Info:

- Info Per Serving: Calories: 220;Fat: 14g;Protein: 4g;Carbs: 25g.

Carrot & Walnut Cake

Servings:6
Cooking Time:55 Minutes

Ingredients:

- ½ cup vegetable oil
- 2 tsp vanilla extract
- ¼ cup maple syrup
- 6 eggs, beaten
- ½ cup flour
- 1 tsp baking powder
- 1 tsp baking soda
- ½ tsp ground nutmeg
- 1 tsp ground cinnamon
- ½ tsp salt
- ½ cup chopped walnuts
- 3 cups finely grated carrots

Directions:

1. Preheat oven to 350 F. Mix the vanilla extract, maple syrup, and oil in a large bowl. Stir to mix well. Add in the eggs and whisk to combine. Set aside.
2. Combine the flour, baking powder, baking soda, nutmeg, cinnamon, and salt in a separate bowl. Stir to combine. Make a well in the center of the flour mixture, then pour the egg mixture into the well and stir well. Add in the walnuts and carrots and toss to mix well. Pour the mixture into a greased baking dish. Bake for 35-45 minutes or until puffed and the cake spring back when lightly press with your fingers. Remove the cake from the oven. Allow to cool, then serve.

Nutrition Info:

Info Per Serving: Calories: 255;Fat: 21g;Protein: .1g;Carbs: 13g.

Mint Raspberries Panna Cotta

Servings:4
Cooking Time:15 Min + Chilling Time

Ingredients:

- 2 tbsp warm water
- 2 tsp gelatin powder
- 2 cups heavy cream
- 1 cup raspberries
- 2 tbsp sugar
- 1 tsp vanilla extract
- 4 fresh mint leaves

Directions:

1. Pour 2 tbsp of warm water into a small bowl. Stir in the gelatin to dissolve. Allow the mixture to sit for 10 minutes. In a large bowl, combine the heavy cream, raspberries, sugar, and vanilla. Blend with an immersion blender until the mixture is smooth and the raspberries are well puréed. Transfer the mixture to a saucepan and heat over medium heat until just below a simmer. Remove from the heat and let cool for 5 minutes. Add in the gelatin mixture, whisking constantly until smooth. Divide the custard between ramekins and refrigerate until set, 4-6 hours. Serve chilled garnished with mint leaves.

Nutrition Info:

- Info Per Serving: Calories: 431;Fat: 44g;Protein: 4g;Carbs: 7g.

Sweet Spiced Pumpkin Pudding

Servings:6
Cooking Time: 0 Minutes

Ingredients:

- 1 cup pure pumpkin purée
- 2 cups unsweetened coconut milk
- 1 teaspoon ground cinnamon
- ¼ teaspoon ground nutmeg
- ½ teaspoon ground ginger
- Pinch cloves
- ¼ cup pure maple syrup
- 2 tablespoons chopped pecans, for garnish

Directions:

1. Combine all the ingredients, except for the chopped pecans, in a large bowl. Stir to mix well.

2. Wrap the bowl in plastic and refrigerate for at least 2 hours.

3. Remove the bowl from the refrigerator and discard the plastic. Spread the pudding with pecans and serve chilled.

Nutrition Info:

• Info Per Serving: Calories: 249;Fat: 21.1g;Protein: 2.8g;Carbs: 17.2g.

Chocolate-avocado Cream

Servings:4
Cooking Time:10 Min + Chilling Time

Ingredients:

• 2 avocados, mashed
• ¼ cup cocoa powder
• ¼ cup heavy whipping cream
• 2 tsp vanilla extract
• 2 tbsp sugar
• ½ tsp ground cinnamon
• ¼ tsp salt

Directions:

1. Blend the avocado, cocoa powder, heavy whipping cream, vanilla, sugar, cinnamon, and salt into a large bowl until smooth and creamy. Cover and refrigerate for at least 1 hour.

Nutrition Info:

• Info Per Serving: Calories: 230;Fat: 22g;Protein: 3g;Carbs: 10g.

Stuffed Cherry Tomatoes

Servings:4
Cooking Time:10 Minutes

Ingredients:

• 2 tbsp olive oil
• 16 cherry tomatoes
• 1 tbsp lemon zest
• ½ cup feta cheese, crumbled
• 2 tbsp olive tapenade
• ¼ cup parsley, torn

Directions:

1. Using a sharp knife, slice off the tops of the tomatoes and hollow out the insides. Combine olive oil, lemon zest, feta cheese, olive tapenade, and parsley in a bowl. Fill the cherry tomatoes with the feta mixture and arrange them on a plate.

Nutrition Info:

• Info Per Serving: Calories: 140;Fat: 9g;Protein: 6g;-Carbs: 6g.

Balsamic Strawberry Caprese Skewers

Servings:6
Cooking Time:15 Min + Cooling Time

Ingredients:

• 1 tbsp olive oil
• 1 cup balsamic vinegar
• 24 whole, hulled strawberries
• 24 basil leaves, halved
• 12 fresh mozzarella balls

Directions:

1. Pour the balsamic vinegar into a small saucepan and simmer for 10 minutes or until it's reduced by half and is thick enough to coat the back of a spoon. Set aside to cool completely. Thread the strawberries onto wooden skewers, followed by basil leaves folded in half and mozzarella balls. Drizzle with balsamic glaze and olive oil and serve.

Nutrition Info:

• Info Per Serving: Calories: 206;Fat: 10g;Protein 10g;Carbs: 17g.

Roasted Veggies With Marsala Sauce

Servings:4
Cooking Time:30 Minutes

Ingredients:

- Vegetables:
- ¼ cup olive oil
- 1 lb green beans, trimmed
- ½ lb carrots, trimmed
- 1 fennel bulb, sliced
- ¼ cup dry white wine
- ¼ tsp oregano
- ½ tsp thyme
- ½ tsp rosemary
- ¼ tsp coriander seeds
- ¼ tsp celery seeds
- ¼ tsp dried dill weed
- 1 head garlic, halved
- 1 red onion, sliced
- Salt and black pepper to taste
- Sauce:
- 2 tbsp olive oil
- 2 tbsp Marsala wine
- 2 tbsp plain yogurt
- 1 tbsp yellow mustard
- 1 tsp honey
- 1 tbsp lemon juice
- 1 yolk from 1 hard-boiled egg
- Salt to taste
- 1 tbsp paprika

Directions:

1. Preheat the oven to 380 F. In a bowl, combine the olive oil, white wine, oregano, thyme, rosemary, coriander seeds, celery seeds, dill weed, salt, and black pepper and mix well. Add in carrots, green beans, fennel, garlic, and onion and toss to coat. Spread the mixture on a baking dish and roast in the oven for 15-20 minutes until tender.

2. In a food processor, place the honey, yogurt, mustard, lemon juice, Marsala wine, yolk, olive oil, salt, and paprika, and blitz until smooth and uniform. Transfer to a bowl and place in the fridge until ready to use. When the veggies are ready, remove and serve with the prepared sauce on the side.

Nutrition Info:

- Info Per Serving: Calories: 280;Fat: 20.2g;Protein: 4g;Carbs: 21g.

Salt & Pepper Toasted Walnuts

Servings:6
Cooking Time:20 Minutes

Ingredients:

- 2 tbsp olive oil
- 4 cups walnut halves
- Sea salt flakes to taste
- Black pepper to taste

Directions:

1. Preheat the oven to 250 F. In a bowl, toss the walnuts with olive oil, salt, and pepper to coat. Spread out the walnuts on a parchment-lined baking sheet. Toast for 10-15 minutes. Remove from the oven and allow to cool completely. Serve.

Nutrition Info:

- Info Per Serving: Calories: 193;Fat: 2g;Protein: 8g;-Carbs: 23g.

Spicy Hummus

Servings:6
Cooking Time:10 Minutes

Ingredients:

- 2 tbsp olive oil
- ½ tsp hot paprika
- 1 tsp hot pepper sauce
- 1 tsp ground cumin
- 3 garlic cloves, minced
- 1 can chickpeas
- 2 tbsp tahini
- 2 tbsp chopped fresh parsley
- 1 lemon, juiced and zested
- Salt to taste

Directions:

1. In a food processor, blend chickpeas, tahini, oil, garlic, lemon juice, lemon zest, salt, cumin, and hot pepper sauce for a minute until smooth. Decorate with parsley and paprika.

Nutrition Info:

- Info Per Serving: Calories: 236;Fat: 8.6g;Protein: 10g;Carbs: 31g.

Crispy Potato Chips

Servings:4
Cooking Time:40 Minutes

Ingredients:

- 2 tbsp olive oil
- 4 potatoes, cut into wedges
- 2 tbsp grated Parmesan cheese
- Salt and black pepper to taste

Directions:

1. Preheat the oven to 340 F. In a bowl, combine the potatoes, olive oil, salt, and black pepper. Spread on a lined baking sheet and bake for 40 minutes until the edges are browned. Serve sprinkled with Parmesan cheese.

Nutrition Info:

- Info Per Serving: Calories: 359;Fat: 8g;Protein: 9g;-Carbs: 66g.

Orange Mug Cakes

Servings:2
Cooking Time: 3 Minutes

Ingredients:

- 6 tablespoons flour
- 2 tablespoons sugar
- 1 teaspoon orange zest
- ½ teaspoon baking powder
- Pinch salt
- 1 egg
- 2 tablespoons olive oil
- 2 tablespoons unsweetened almond milk
- 2 tablespoons freshly squeezed orange juice
- ½ teaspoon orange extract
- ½ teaspoon vanilla extract

Directions:

1. Combine the flour, sugar, orange zest, baking powder, and salt in a small bowl.
2. In another bowl, whisk together the egg, olive oil, milk, orange juice, orange extract, and vanilla extract.
3. Add the dry ingredients to the wet ingredients and

stir to incorporate. The batter will be thick.
4. Divide the mixture into two small mugs. Microwave each mug separately. The small ones should take about 60 seconds, and one large mug should take about 90 seconds, but microwaves can vary.
5. Cool for 5 minutes before serving.

Nutrition Info:

- Info Per Serving: Calories: 303;Fat: 16.9g;Protein: 6.0g;Carbs: 32.5g.

Lemony Tea And Chia Pudding

Servings:3
Cooking Time: 0 Minutes

Ingredients:

- 2 teaspoons matcha green tea powder (optional)
- 2 tablespoons ground chia seeds
- 1 to 2 dates
- 2 cups unsweetened coconut milk
- Zest and juice of 1 lime

Directions:

1. Put all the ingredients in a food processor and pulse until creamy and smooth.
2. Pour the mixture in a bowl, then wrap in plastic. Store in the refrigerator for at least 20 minutes, then serve chilled.

Nutrition Info:

- Info Per Serving: Calories: 225;Fat: 20.1g;Protein: 3.2g;Carbs: 5.9g.

Hummus & Tomato Stuffed Cucumbers

Servings:2
Cooking Time:5 Minutes

Ingredients:

- 1 cucumber, halved lengthwise
- ½ cup hummus
- 5 cherry tomatoes, halved
- 2 tbsp fresh basil, minced

Directions:

1. Using a paring knife, scoop most of the seeds from the inside of each cucumber piece to make a cup, bein

careful not to cut all the way through. Fill each cucumber cup with about 1 tablespoon of hummus. Top with cherry tomatoes and basil.

Nutrition Info:

- Info Per Serving: Calories: 135;Fat: 6g;Protein: 6g;-Carbs: 16g.

Fresh Fruit Cups

Servings:4
Cooking Time:10 Minutes

Ingredients:

- 1 cup orange juice
- ½ cup watermelon cubes
- 1 ½ cups grapes, halved
- 1 cup chopped cantaloupe
- ½ cup cherries, chopped
- 1 peach, chopped
- ½ tsp ground cinnamon

Directions:

1. Combine watermelon cubes, grapes, cherries, cantaloupe, and peach in a bowl. Add in the orange juice and mix well. Share into dessert cups, dust with cinnamon, and serve.

Nutrition Info:

- Info Per Serving: Calories: 156;Fat: 0.5g;Protein: 1.8g;Carbs: 24g.

Two-cheese Stuffed Bell Peppers

Servings:6
Cooking Time:20 Min + Chilling Time

Ingredients:

- 1 ½ lb bell peppers, cored and seeded
- 1 tbsp extra-virgin olive oil
- 4 oz ricotta cheese
- 4 oz mascarpone cheese
- 1 tbsp scallions, chopped
- 1 tbsp lemon zest

Directions:

1. Preheat oven to 400 F. Coat the peppers with olive oil, put them on a baking sheet, and roast for 8 minutes. Remove and let cool. In a bowl, add the ricotta cheese, mascarpone cheese, scallions, and lemon zest. Stir to combine, then spoon mixture into a piping bag. Stuff each pepper to the top with the cheese mixture. Chill the peppers and serve.

Nutrition Info:

- Info Per Serving: Calories: 141;Fat: 11g;Protein: 4g;Carbs: 6g.

Spiced Fries

Servings:6
Cooking Time:35 Minutes

Ingredients:

- 2 lb red potatoes, cut into wedges
- ¼ cup olive oil
- 3 tbsp garlic, minced
- ½ tsp smoked paprika
- Salt and black pepper to taste
- ½ cup fresh cilantro, chopped
- ¼ tsp cayenne pepper

Directions:

1. Preheat oven to 450 F. Place the potatoes into a bowl. Add the garlic, salt, pepper, and olive oil and toss everything together to coat evenly. Spread the potato mixture onto a baking sheet; bake for 25 minutes, flipping them halfway through the cooking time until golden and crisp. Sprinkle the potatoes with cilantro, cayenne pepper, and smoked paprika. Serve warm and enjoy!

Nutrition Info:

- Info Per Serving: Calories: 203;Fat: 11g;Protein: 3g;Carbs: 24g.

Spicy Roasted Chickpeas

Servings:2
Cooking Time:40 Minutes

Ingredients:

- Chickpeas
- 1 tbsp olive oil
- 1 can chickpeas
- Salt to taste
- Seasoning Mix
- ¾ tsp cumin

- ½ tsp ground coriander
- Salt and black pepper to taste
- ¼ tsp chili powder
- ½ tsp cayenne pepper
- ¼ tsp cardamom
- ¼ tsp cinnamon
- ¼ tsp allspice

Directions:

1. Preheat oven to 400 F. In a small bowl, place all the seasoning mix ingredients and stir well to combine.

2. Place the chickpeas in a bowl and season them with olive oil and salt. Add the chickpeas to a lined baking sheet and roast them for about 25-35 minutes, turning them over once or twice while cooking until they are slightly crisp. Remove to a bowl and sprinkle them with the seasoning mix. Toss lightly to combine. Serve and enjoy!

Nutrition Info:

- Info Per Serving: Calories: 268;Fat: 11g;Protein: 11g;Carbs: 35g.

Cheese Stuffed Potato Skins

Servings:4
Cooking Time:40 Minutes

Ingredients:

- 2 tbsp olive oil
- 1 lb red baby potatoes
- 1 cup ricotta cheese, crumbled
- 2 garlic cloves, minced
- 1 tbsp chives, chopped
- ½ tsp hot chili sauce
- Salt and black pepper to taste

Directions:

1. Place potatoes and enough water in a pot over medium heat and bring to a boil. Simmer for 15 minutes and drain. Let them cool. Cut them in halves and scoop out the pulp. Place the pulp in a bowl and mash it a bit with a fork. Add in the ricotta cheese, olive oil, garlic, chives, chili sauce, salt, and pepper. Mix to combine. Fill potato skins with the mixture.

2. Preheat oven to 360 F. Line a baking sheet with parchment paper. Place filled skins on the sheet and bake for 10 minutes.

Nutrition Info:

- Info Per Serving: Calories: 310;Fat: 10g;Protein: 9g;Carbs: 23g.

Home-style Trail Mix

Servings:4
Cooking Time:30 Minutes

Ingredients:

- 1 cup dried apricots, cut into thin strips
- 2 tbsp olive oil
- 1 cup pepitas
- 1 cup walnut halves
- 1 cup dried dates, chopped
- 1 cup golden raisins
- 1 cup raw almonds
- 1 tsp salt

Directions:

1. Preheat the oven to 310 F. Combine almonds, pepitas, dates, walnuts, apricots, and raisins in a bowl. Mix in olive oil and salt and toss to coat. Spread the mixture on a lined with parchment paper sheet, and bake for 30 minutes or until the fruits are slightly browned. Let to cool before serving.

Nutrition Info:

- Info Per Serving: Calories: 267;Fat: 14g;Protein: 7g;Carbs: 35g.

Vanilla Cheesecake Squares

Servings:6
Cooking Time:55 Min + Chilling Time

Ingredients:

- ½ cup butter, melted
- 1 box butter cake mix
- 3 large eggs
- 1 cup maple syrup
- 1/8 tsp cinnamon
- 1 cup cream cheese
- 1 tsp vanilla extract

Directions:

1. Preheat oven to 350 F. In a medium bowl, blend the cake mix, butter, cinnamon, and 1 egg. Then, pour th

mixture into a greased baking pan. Mix together maple syrup, cream cheese, the remaining 2 eggs, and vanilla in a separate bowl and pour this gently over the first layer. Bake for 45-50 minutes. Remove and allow to cool. Cut into squares.

Nutrition Info:

• Info Per Serving: Calories: 160;Fat: 8g;Protein: 2g;-Carbs: 20g.

Crunchy Almond Cookies

Servings:4
Cooking Time: 5 To 7 Minutes

Ingredients:

• ½ cup sugar
• 8 tablespoons almond butter
• 1 large egg
• 1½ cups all-purpose flour
• 1 cup ground almonds

Directions:

1. Preheat the oven to 375ºF. Line a baking sheet with parchment paper.
2. Using a mixer, whisk together the sugar and butter. Add the egg and mix until combined. Alternately add the flour and ground almonds, ½ cup at a time, while the mixer is on slow.
3. Drop 1 tablespoon of the dough on the prepared baking sheet, keeping the cookies at least 2 inches apart.
4. Put the baking sheet in the oven and bake for about 5 to 7 minutes, or until the cookies start to turn brown around the edges.
5. Let cool for 5 minutes before serving.

Nutrition Info:

• Info Per Serving: Calories: 604;Fat: 36.0g;Protein: 11.0g;Carbs: 63.0g.

Turkish Dolma (stuffed Grape Leaves)

Servings:4
Cooking Time:50 Minutes

Ingredients:

• 2 tbsp olive oil
• 1 onion, chopped
• 2 garlic cloves, minced
• 1 cup short-grain rice
• ¼ cup gold raisins
• ¼ cup pine nuts, toasted
• 1 lemon, juiced
• ¼ tsp ground cinnamon
• Salt and black pepper to taste
• 2 tbsp parsley, chopped
• 20 preserved grape leaves

Directions:

1. Warm the olive oil in a skillet over medium heat. Add the onion and garlic and sauté for 5 minutes. Add the rice, golden raisins, pine nuts, cinnamon, and lemon juice. Season with salt and pepper. Stuff each leaf with about 1 tablespoon of the filling. Roll tightly and place each in a pot, seam side down. Add 2 cups of water and simmer for about 15-18 minutes. Serve warm.

Nutrition Info:

• Info Per Serving: Calories: 237;Fat: 12g;Protein: 7g;Carbs: 26g.

No-gluten Caprese Pizza

Servings:4
Cooking Time:40 Minutes

Ingredients:

• 2 tbsp olive oil
• 2 ¼ cups chickpea flour
• Salt and black pepper to taste
• 1 tsp onion powder
• 1 tomato, sliced
• ¼ tsp dried oregano
• 2 oz mozzarella cheese, sliced
• ¼ cup tomato sauce
• 2 tbsp fresh basil, chopped

Directions:

1. Preheat oven to 360 F. Combine the chickpea flour, salt, pepper, 1 ¼ cups of water, olive oil, and onion powder in a bowl. Mix well to form a soft dough, then knead a bit until elastic. Let sit covered in a greased bowl to rise, for 25 minutes in a warm place. Remove the dough to a floured surface and roll out it with a rolling pin into a thin circle.

2. Transfer to a floured baking tray and bake in the oven for 10 minutes. Evenly spread the tomato sauce over the pizza base. Sprinkle with oregano and arrange the mozzarella cheese and tomato slices on top. Bake for 10 minutes. Top with basil and serve sliced.

Nutrition Info:

• Info Per Serving: Calories: 420;Fat: 26g;Protein: 14g;Carbs: 35g.

Spanish-style Pizza With Jamón Serrano

Servings:4
Cooking Time:90 Minutes

Ingredients:

• For the crust
• 2 tbsp olive oil
• 2 cups flour
• 1 cup lukewarm water
• 1 pinch of sugar
• 1 tsp active dry yeast
• ¾ tsp salt
• For the topping
• 1/3 cup Spanish olives with pimento
• ½ cup tomato sauce
• ½ cup sliced mozzarella
• 4 oz jamon serrano, sliced
• 7 fresh basil leaves

Directions:

1. Sift the flour and salt in a bowl and stir in yeast. Mix lukewarm water, olive oil, and sugar in another bowl. Add the wet mixture to the dry mixture and whisk until you obtain a soft dough. Place the dough on a lightly floured work surface and knead it thoroughly for 4-5 minutes until elastic. Transfer the dough to a greased bowl. Cover with cling film and leave to rise for 50-60 minutes in a warm place until doubled

in size. Roll out the dough to a thickness of around 12 inches.

2. Preheat the oven to 400 F. Line a pizza pan with parchment paper. Spread the tomato sauce on the crust. Arrange the mozzarella slices on the sauce and then the Jamon serrano. Bake for 15 minutes or until the cheese melts. Remove from the oven and top with olives and basil. Slice and serve warm.

Nutrition Info:

• Info Per Serving: Calories: 160;Fat: 6g;Protein: 22g;Carbs: 0.5g.

Cinnamon Pear & Oat Crisp With Pecans

Servings:4
Cooking Time:30 Minutes

Ingredients:

• 2 tbsp butter, melted
• 4 fresh pears, mashed
• ½ lemon, juiced and zested
• ¼ cup maple syrup
• 1 cup gluten-free rolled oats
• ½ cup chopped pecans
• ½ tsp ground cinnamon
• ¼ tsp salt

Directions:

1. Preheat oven to 350 F. Combine the pears, lemon juice and zest, and maple syrup in a bowl. Stir to mix well, then spread the mixture on a greased baking dish. Combine the remaining ingredients in a small bowl. Stir to mix well. Pour the mixture over the pear mixture. Bake for 20 minutes or until the oats are golden brown.

Nutrition Info:

• Info Per Serving: Calories: 496;Fat: 33g;Protein: 5g;Carbs: 50.8g.

Simple Spiced Sweet Pecans

Servings:4
Cooking Time: 17 Minutes

Ingredients:

- 1 cup pecan halves
- 3 tablespoons almond butter
- 1 teaspoon ground cinnamon
- ½ teaspoon ground nutmeg
- ¼ cup raw honey
- ¼ teaspoon sea salt

Directions:

1. Preheat the oven to 350°F. Line a baking sheet with parchment paper.
2. Combine all the ingredients in a bowl. Stir to mix well, then spread the mixture in the single layer on the baking sheet with a spatula.
3. Bake in the preheated oven for 16 minutes or until the pecan halves are well browned.
4. Serve immediately.

Nutrition Info:

- Info Per Serving: Calories: 324;Fat: 29.8g;Protein: 3.2g;Carbs: 13.9g.

Cherry & Almond Bulgur Bowl

Servings:6
Cooking Time:20 Minutes

Ingredients:

- 1 tbsp vanilla sugar
- 1 ½ cups bulgur
- 2 cups milk
- 1 cup water
- ½ tsp ground cinnamon
- 2 cups cherries, pitted
- 8 dried figs, chopped
- ½ cup almonds, chopped
- ¼ cup fresh mint, chopped

Directions:

1. Combine the vanilla sugar, bulgur, milk, cinnamon, and 1 cup of water in a medium pot and stir to dissolve the sugar. Bring just to a boil. Cover, reduce the heat to medium-low, and simmer for 10 minutes or until the liquid is absorbed.
2. Turn off the heat and stir in the cherries, figs, and almonds. Cover and let the hot bulgur thaw the cherries and partially hydrate the figs. Top with mint. Serve chilled or hot.

Nutrition Info:

- Info Per Serving: Calories: 207;Fat: 6g;Protein: 8g;-Carbs: 32g.

APPENDIX A: Measurement Conversions

BASIC KITCHEN CONVERSIONS & EQUIVALENTS

DRY MEASUREMENTS CONVERSION CHART

3 TEASPOONS = 1 TABLESPOON = 1/16 CUP

6 TEASPOONS = 2 TABLESPOONS = 1/8 CUP

12 TEASPOONS = 4 TABLESPOONS = 1/4 CUP

24 TEASPOONS = 8 TABLESPOONS = 1/2 CUP

36 TEASPOONS = 12 TABLESPOONS = 3/4 CUP

48 TEASPOONS = 16 TABLESPOONS = 1 CUP

METRIC TO US COOKING CONVERSIONS

OVEN TEMPERATURES

120 °C = 250 °F

160 °C = 320 °F

180° C = 350 °F

205 °C = 400 °F

220 °C = 425 °F

LIQUID MEASUREMENTS CONVERSION CHART

8 FLUID OUNCES = 1 CUP = 1/2 PINT = 1/4 QUART

16 FLUID OUNCES = 2 CUPS = 1 PINT = 1/2 QUART

32 FLUID OUNCES = 4 CUPS = 2 PINTS = 1 QUART

= 1/4 GALLON

128 FLUID OUNCES = 16 CUPS = 8 PINTS = 4 QUARTS = 1 GALLON

BAKING IN GRAMS

1 CUP FLOUR = 140 GRAMS

1 CUP SUGAR = 150 GRAMS

1 CUP POWDERED SUGAR = 160 GRAMS

1 CUP HEAVY CREAM = 235 GRAMS

VOLUME

1 MILLILITER = 1/5 TEASPOON

5 ML = 1 TEASPOON

15 ML = 1 TABLESPOON

240 ML = 1 CUP OR 8 FLUID OUNCES

1 LITER = 34 FL. OUNCES

WEIGHT

1 GRAM = .035 OUNCES

100 GRAMS = 3.5 OUNCES

500 GRAMS = 1.1 POUNDS

1 KILOGRAM = 35 OUNCES

US TO METRIC COOKING CONVERSIONS

1/5 TSP = 1 ML

1 TSP = 5 ML

1 TBSP = 15 ML

1 FL OUNCE = 30 ML

1 CUP = 237 ML

1 PINT (2 CUPS) = 473 ML

1 QUART (4 CUPS) = .95 LITER

1 GALLON (16 CUPS) = 3.8 LITERS

1 OZ = 28 GRAMS

1 POUND = 454 GRAMS

BUTTER

1 CUP BUTTER = 2 STICKS = 8 OUNCES = 230 GRAMS = 8 TABLESPOONS

WHAT DOES 1 CUP EQUAL

1 CUP = 8 FLUID OUNCES

1 CUP = 16 TABLESPOONS

1 CUP = 48 TEASPOONS

1 CUP = 1/2 PINT

1 CUP = 1/4 QUART

1 CUP = 1/16 GALLON

1 CUP = 240 ML

BAKING PAN CONVERSIONS

1 CUP ALL-PURPOSE FLOUR = 4.5 OZ

1 CUP ROLLED OATS = 3 OZ 1 LARGE EGG = 1.7 OZ

1 CUP BUTTER = 8 OZ 1 CUP MILK = 8 OZ

1 CUP HEAVY CREAM = 8.4 OZ

1 CUP GRANULATED SUGAR = 7.1 OZ

1 CUP PACKED BROWN SUGAR = 7.75 OZ

1 CUP VEGETABLE OIL = 7.7 OZ

1 CUP UNSIFTED POWDERED SUGAR = 4.4 OZ

BAKING PAN CONVERSIONS

9-INCH ROUND CAKE PAN = 12 CUPS

10-INCH TUBE PAN =16 CUPS

11-INCH BUNDT PAN = 12 CUPS

9-INCH SPRINGFORM PAN = 10 CUPS

9 X 5 INCH LOAF PAN = 8 CUPS

9-INCH SQUARE PAN = 8 CUPS

Appendix B : Recipes Index

S

T

Made in the USA
Las Vegas, NV
15 September 2023

77601266R00057